The Surviv...
For th...

BEATING
Burnout

Peter McGugan Ct. H.,H.B.J.,B.A.

Edited by Dr. Irene Hickman

CATALOGING IN PUBLICATION DATA

McGugan, Peter M. [Peter Malcolm), 1956 -
Beating Burnout: the survival guide for the 90s

Includes index
ISBN 0-9694312-0-1

1. Burnout 2. Business Stress 3. Self Help 4. Stress [psychology]

Editor: Dr. Irene Hickman
Cover Design and Illustration: Grag Salmela
Cover Photos: Ross Breadner Photography
Burnout Wheel Calculations: Herb Mackenzie
Cartoons: Peter McGugan

Commonwealth First Edition   Jan. 1990
Commonwealth Second Edition   June 1990
Commonwealth Third Edition   September 1990
U.S. First Edition Feb. 1991
U.S. Second Edition August 1991

Printed on
Recycled Paper

published by
Potentials Press
P.O. 24042 London, Ontario, Canada   N6H 5C4
(519) 645-0884   (214) 987-3123

Dedication

To Khyle, Linda, Greg
Lucille, Celeste, Loretta

and
the humanization of Life.

Table Of Contents

Introduction

Whether you thrive on work or it thrives on you, sucking your energy and draining your passion, you are in control. Everyone can beat burnout with the proper tools and perspective on work.

In this Western society work is much more than a source of income, it is a source of identity, the sound of your voice joining in the cacophony of human endeavor. Do you sense the noise getting louder, more deafening?

Surveys indicate we're now working harder than we did five years ago. The numbers of people working more than fifty hours a week is rapidly increasing, and there is every evidence that in the next decade the pressures will mount. In the 1990s the pace is set by more distant factors, economic competition from a newly united European Community, from the Pacific rim and free trade. These factors affect us all. As business people experience increased competition, greater distancing between markets and the perception of the planet being a global shopping mall, burnout is dramatically increasing. Those who become sick and tired put tremendous pressure on co-workers, families, social agencies, police, caregivers and so on.

Many of us love our career, the question is when the year 2,000 arrives, will you have survived your career intact?

Consider the future, increased competition on personal and corporate levels, longer commutes, leaner companies, more two career families. As we mall the planet, companies merge and change, grow and wither; many of us live with greater uncertainty in every facet of our lives. This perceived lack of control smothers passion.

Work used to have dimension: nine to five Monday to Friday. The rest of the time was yours, but in the 90s there are fewer and fewer escapes. Technology is extending the chain from your desk to your ankle and it will not be a ball. Think about faxes that chase you and pagers that join people at the hip vibrating silently to notify you during concerts, intimate dinners or funerals.

Work can refuse containment, like a colorless odorless gas, we breath it everywhere.

The future work pace will leave us feeling sometimes exhilarated but most of the time anxious, frustrated, stressed and unsure of where it all leads.

As burnout takes its grip we lurch into the next moment fleetingly aware that if we raise our nose from the grindstone we might be in for a shocking surprise. And so we don't.

We have a work force of people juggling a dozen things, in search of fulfillment and passion and feeling they're not doing anything particularly well. Parts of the job may be interesting but there isn't time to enjoy it.

We were taught hard work and hanging-in-there would give us a foot up, but many of us are hanging by our finger nails.

Lights On The Horizon

Those in touch with their wants, needs and values are leading the way out of the busy-ness abyss. Some employers are accepting flexible hours and *clear times* to do Life tasks like ferrying a child or caring for an elderly parent. Both males and females are taking leaves of absence to become parents.

America is slowly becoming more humanized, absenteeism for family reasons has doubled in recent years. As problems at work lead to problems at home and visa versa, the need to escape and nurture the Self or a loved one must be requested, granted and accepted without guilt.

The companies tuned into the humanization of America

understand it is better to grant employees a few hours off for Life issues than have them lie, say they are sick and take a whole day off.

Greater workplace flexibility is a reality in the 1990s but the people who need it most will not use it. The highly educated, professional, often well paid, white male, will not use the tools for beating burnout until the physical, emotional or spiritual signals are debilitating. When this happens everybody has lost and continues to lose. When four alarm burnout hits, other employees, spouses and children are already victims.

People obsessed with moving up the ladder, whose Self worth begins and ends with professional achievement will continue to bop until they drop because the choice jobs require always being available.

The value our society sets on moving up comes from a post-war model, a generation sucked up into positions of prosperity. Younger people who witnessed the rapid ascents of post war "success models" refuse to be happy where they are, but times have changed. The baby boomers are clinging to very crowded ladders and those further up aren't getting out of the way fast enough. Many boomers are finally arriving at middle management positions just as those jobs are being trimmed away. Their reaction is to work harder because their version of success is to have it all and that means conspicuous consumption just to "stay in the game".

It requires honest soul searching for corporate achievers to realize the unhappiness comes, not from the job, but from their narrow personal agendas and expectations. They're putting off happiness until something that is unlikely to happen happens. They spin their wheels trying to get somewhere that may not exist...trying to get anywhere, falling behind as they're getting ahead. If they make the dream happen what has been sacrificed, Self esteem, health, family?

The bravado of complaining and boasting about how hard you work, how many hours you put in and the perks, quirks and smirks of the job is a symptom of people convincing themselves that they can take it.

Success and fulfillment are slippery beasts to snare if Cosmic significance is pinned on a job fantasy.

In the turbulent years ahead, it is only by snaring the Self and spending some quiet time slaying the inner beasts that we will beat burnout and master the lessons of Life.

Chapter 1:   Burnout Symptoms

It has to do with passion. When the passion is burning within us we're motivated, excited and capable. Traditionally, when we begin something new, whether it be a career, a job or a relationship, we enter with a burning passion. And that passion lifts and carries us through the day and night, because we are learning, growing and we're experiencing that wonderful feeling of fulfillment.

We value what we're doing and the energy that we put into doing it comes back to us in the form of fulfillment. We're being stretched, experiencing new sensations and interactions and we're alive!

So what happens? Where does the passion go? Why do people who are active, intelligent achievers reach states of ineffectiveness, fatigue and frustration leading to total shut-down?We need to ask ourself, am I burning out and what can I do to keep myself in a state of steady fuel, steady performance for ongoing health, wealth and well being?   This book is designed to lead to those answers and more.

The word burnout evokes images of a final flickering flame, of a charred and empty shell, of dying embers and cold ashes. Like fire, motivation gets stronger, burns hot and with the proper delivery of fuel can stay hot, or if conditions change the fire fades. Even the hottest fires burn out, we know it is necessary to tend a fire, to fan it , fuel it, give it oxygen, clean out the ash buildup and on occasion add another log.

Like fires, people are not static: When fuel or motivation wanes, we burnout. Yet there is no cause for panic. We've built the fire before, as long as we can gather fuel and clean away the old ash the flame can burn brightly again.

No one is immune. Anyone in any profession at any level can burnout. But the people at highest risk work closely with people, dealing with emotional, social and health problems.

Loss of enthusiasm and interest, translate into major problems in the workplace and at home. Burnout symptoms have been blamed for costing the North American economy 200 billion dollars every year. <u>One major North American car company pays as much for stress and burnout as it does for steel.</u> The effects of burnout are devastating to families. We only have to look at drug abuse, alcoholism, spouse and child abuse, suicides and other Self abuse to see evidence of people who've lost their passion, their joy, their Self control and Self Love.

By dealing with the causes of burnout we deal with the same issues that cause the burnout symptoms of our society.

The Time Famine

Time is to the 90s what money was to the 80s. Pollster Louis Harris charted America's loss of time in the late 80s and concluded "Time may have become the most precious commodity in the land." Acceleration is not just an impression. According to a Harris survey the amount of leisure time enjoyed by the average American shrunk 37% between 1973 & 1989. Over the same period the average work week, including commuting, increased by 20%.

So how did we become so timeless? In the 70s computers, satellites, robotics and other wizardries promised to make Life so much more efficient, production and incomes were supposed to rise while the work week shrank. In 1967 a U.S. senate subcommittee was told that our great challenge by the year 1995 would be to find ways of enjoying all our leisure time.

The computers are byting, the satellites spinning and the microwaves waving, but we are out of breath. In a culture so committed to saving time we're missing the prize we lunge for. We may find ourselves talking about relaxation the way a hungry person talks about food.

We've given up the ease of living for a merchandized life-style fashioned by the advertisers of pop culture. Styling a Life is very expensive.

The technology that was supposed to break the chains of work has in fact increased our heartbeats, binding the planet with a global economy and too many market opportunities to miss. We use computers that work for us in a trillionth of a second. Try catching your breath in a trillionth of a second.

Information breeds information and it explodes daily, leaving us with too many new facts to miss, and far too many to absorb. Rather than stopping, turning to face the monster and shouting, "HEY this isn't what was supposed to happen", we're chased by a work ethic that is on the surface trendy but is really quite mad.

The cost of a home has soared, inflation erodes paychecks and wages are rather stagnant, in the big cities it usually takes two paychecks to fund a middle-class life. The American dream is still intact, it just costs a lot more.

When both mother and father work to make ends meet Life issues like making lunches, parenting, shopping, cooking, repairing, laundering and driving still need to be done. The loss of the full time homemaker has done more to erode our leisure time than any other factor. "Quality time" with loved ones needs to be scheduled. Many of the Life chores are contracted out, but eventually you have more of an enterprise than a family.

Burning out doesn't lead us away from Life, it leads us back to it.

The causes of burnout vary within different professions. Although one section of this book will apply more directly to you, reading the other sections can give further insight into yourself and others.

I have capitalized the words Self, Life and Love. It amazes me that we capitalize the names of cities, towns, villages and hamlets, lakes, rivers and even streets, but we do not always capitalize Earth, Universe or Cosmos. And we do not capitalize Life or Love. I do, because I think they're important enough. The Self I describe by capitalizing is the amazing and wonderful essence of you created by a master architectural force that doesn't make any junk.

The Burnout Feeling

It can be a feeling of emotional taughtness, as if the slightest inconvenience will make you explode. Like an overloaded electrical circuit, the fuse blows with any additional demand of energy. This can be caused by carrying around heavy energy, frustration, guilt, anger at Self and others, it's not feeling good inside. Dealing with other people, dealing with anybody, is precarious. Dealing with yourSelf is like walking a tight rope. Tolerance levels drop, apathy bleaches out passion, sick and tired is a common state and shut down occurs.

Frustration

Life is a constant state of deciding, a path of sharp edged challenges that can be fraught with frustration. In small doses frustration can be a positive energy, spurring us on to be wise, aware and creative. But when frustration is a constant companion resulting from situations we feel are continual and unsolvable, the stage is set for feelings of futility: "Why bother? They won't appreciate it. There's no point. It's hopeless. I can't do anything anyway."

Feelings of frustration are the first symptom of burnout. Most frustration stems from conflicts and barriers.

Like a weed, frustration grows, spreading feelings of dissatisfaction into other areas of Life, and that original problem can fertilize all those weeds until you're choking.

Many victims of burnout blame their own feelings for the frustrations. A critical care nurse said, "I became a nurse to help people, to be there as they heal and I don't see much healing. I see pain and fear, there is so much to do, I rarely have time to spend with the patients. I rarely feel satisfied I've done enough. The frustrations of not being able to help and not being appreciated for trying leave me weak."

A defense attorney explains, "I'm here to help these people. They have serious problems and I'm supposed to get them a lighter or suspended sentence. Sometimes I don't devote myself to working out as good a defense as I should. I have a lot of tough, demanding cases and when one of my clients gets a bad deal in a courtroom it nags at me. I often wonder if I've done enough."

A government employee responsible for the safety standards of commercial food explains, "I'm caught between the world of business and the bureaucracy of government and neither understands the needs of the other. My supervisors make uninformed decisions and when I tell them it won't wash with business people they tell me to make it wash. Then I present the new policy to the people and they look at me like I'm the one who is nuts. I'm caught in between two huge walls and I'm the one who gets squeezed. I'm the one who's most interested in the public's safety. My job is important but I don't know how to do it well. I often feel I'm failing."

Nagging guilts fertilize frustration. When people are not given the time or tools they need to do the job they often blame themselves as causes of the problem.

Personal Problems

The frustration weed follows us home where the seeds can spread. Moodiness and irritability over little things are a burnout signal. If communication and tenderness with Self and the special people in Life break down, the frustration seeds are beginning to grow.

Emotional Withdrawl

People often defend themselves against an unpleasant situation by withdrawing their emotions. If it doesn't feel good, then I'll stop myself from feeling. We all have this ability to disconnect the conscious mind from the emotions of the subconscious and soul. We simply pull the plug. Males are often taught to shut down their emotional Self because in our western societies, where men are groomed to be warriors in battle and business, emotions are thought to be a feminine trait, a weakness.

Shutting down emotions is a short term solution. We are feeling beings and if emotions are not acknowledged and released they accumulate in various parts of the body, acting as energy blocks.

Massage therapists are taught to deal with people who vent emotion. People who expect to have a pleasant, tension releasing experience often experience surges of emotion. We store emotions in the tissues of our body. Tight muscles, cramps, skin problems, arthritis, cancer or nervous disorders can be symptoms of repressed emotions. Freud said "Eighty percent of all emotional and physical illness is a result of repression." Many things Freud said have been discounted but this statement is not one of them.

We are feeling, caring human beings. To block emotions is to block humanity. It is interesting that emotional withdrawl is common among people who work in the humanities. Social workers, therapists, psychologists, teachers, lawyers, nurses and police officers commonly experience emotional withdrawl. It is a natural response to the emotional demands placed on the helping professions. Indifference to the plights and problems of other people can be a comfortable insulation for a while.

Dehumanization is another form of emotional withdrawl. Many helpers refer to people as objects, others become aloof and intellectual, talking about people as abstract cases too large to fit into a test tube.

All of these attempts to cope accelerate the burnout process. Often the repression of emotion emerges as hostility, drug abuse, self destructive acts, alcoholism, dis-ease or love abuse. Incidents of wife and child abuse are very high among the helping professions, particularly police officers.

Emotional withdrawl doesn't work. People who are

drawn to work in the helping professions are caring, nurturing people. To withdraw emotions is to deny humanity. Ultimately all we can ever hope to be is human.

Depression

"I don't feel good about myself, I'm tired all the time. I have all kinds of negative feelings. I hate my clients and I hate myself for feeling that way. I can't seem to look forward to anything. It's a major effort to get up and make it through the day. I dread Monday morning."

Battling repressed feelings of negativity and futility can dampen anyone's spirit. The conflict leads to emotional and spiritual exhaustion and feelings of profound depression.

Depression is always repressed anger that makes us feel depleted, low on fuel, and without the strength to find more fuel. Depression may have begun as a response to an isolated situation that planted weeds and thorny feelings within, but the depression itself becomes a steady downpour that dampens the flame. It is a new problem in itself that can suppress the immune system and pull anyone down.

Physical Complaints

"I used to think of myself as a healthy person but these days if there is a bug going around I'm sure to get it, This winter I've already had three colds. Hell, I've had the same cold all winter long, and indigestion too! But what's bothering me most is the insomnia. Maybe one night a week I'll sleep through, but the rest of the time I toss and turn constantly. I can't get the problems out of my head, if I could just shut it all down and get some rest. I've been waking up beat so the day starts off in a slump and I don't get out of it."

Frustration, guilt, fear, anger and conflict are all stressors. The heavy energy of these emotions does weigh heavily on mind or chest or wherever else you may bury it.

Too many people carry grudges, and grudges are thorny, prickly things. Burnout victims carry more than their share of excess emotional baggage. Remember, the root of the word disease is dis - ease.

Drugs

"It started because of work. I was so demoralized, despondent, really. I couldn't sleep. I'd be miserable, thinking about things at work, lying awake for hours and would be exhausted in the morning. I talked to my doctor and he gave me some kind of pill to perk me up. It worked I guess, but I couldn't sleep cause of the pill, so he gave me sleeping pills. Now I'm totally caught in this thing, I need pills to wake up and get through the day and pills to sleep... it's killing me."

As the "blahs" become chronic, many burnouts seek chemical solutions. This includes alcohol, tranquilizers, mood lifters, tobacco or large amounts of coffee, sugar or food.

These short-term solutions become a new weed that chokes passion. They put an added strain on an already weakened biological system, aggravating the original problem and creating a whole new set of disfunctions to deal with.

Poor Performance And "Screw Ups"

Peak performance requires high energy, good health and enthusiasm - all are depleted by burnout. When burnout begins, work becomes painful and less rewarding, then resentment sets in. Even when physically at work the burnout victim is often mentally or emotionally absent.

"When I first started the business I was a red-hot go-getter. I was passionate about it. I ate it, slept it, loved it, I married it, which upset the woman I'd previously married. But this was my chance, my shot at doing something. Things weren't easy. I had a lot to learn, had to refinance, and I got run down. I started to resent it, the frustrations and demands. I didn't feel like the same person any more and I stopped caring as much. I cared less and less. I'd burned out. The quality of work dropped, I wasn't as good with the customers, in fact I was often angry with them. I was depleted. It all took me down - and out. If I'd balanced my life, like my wife told me to, I think I would have been able to hang in, but I gave it all too fast. I was in too big a hurry."

Small business owners are at high risk for burnout yet they are least likely to get help. They're so busy running the show they've stopped running their Life. Too often they learn the hard way that Life is IT! If you're good at Life everything else falls into place.

Vast numbers of people are operating at diminished capacity, in a state of semi burnout. There is little passion, adventure or purpose they can find from their Life experience.

Burnout is often mistaken for the Peter Principle - "*In a hierarchy every employee tends to rise to his level of incompetence*". Because burnout is not always immediately obvious a person may just be functioning in a diminished capacity. The person coasts, doing as little as possible, in many cases simply following the rules. Potential creativity is replaced by rules from the book. Rules provide a shield from responsibility - the ability to respond. Bad situations stay bad and get worse because "I can't help it, I haven't got a choice. These are the rules." In the process the burnout victim loses the ability to deal with individual situations and personalities and eliminates potentials for creative solutions, innovation

<u>and progress for the organization</u>. The subtle consequences of burnout may not be felt immediately but they create serious problems over the long run. A burnt out manager contributes to the burnout of a staff.

Loss Of A Love

The pressure doesn't have to start at work. The difficulties may start at home. Frustrating, conflicting relationships put a strain on your emotional circuits, mixing you up and making you feel unsettled, frustrated or angry. The loss of a relationship through separation or death, or the loss of a child, can nearly extinguish your flame.

Often we don't allow ourselves time to heal when Love hurts. We forget that we are emotionally ill and need tender loving care.

The pain of loss can be deadened with more work, drugs, booze or other Self abuses but pain remains. We must feel our way through the rocky and tender paths of our emotions, we must mourn and cry, nurture and heal with Love and forgiveness and time. Emotions are things, they must be felt in order to be released. Tranquilizers may pull the plug on emotional hurts but the emotions remain, fester and back up within us. The emotional pressure mounts and often hits hard over the slightest little things. We lose control like never before, wondering where all this rage is coming from.

It takes time to become emotionally well after a traumatic loss, yet the thing many people do is go right back to work, ignoring the child within that needs to hurt, cry and forgive.

As a therapist there is something I know about people, <u>we're all after the same things, to be loved and accepted.</u> I've never met a person who isn't wanting to be loved and accepted, I've seen people who go after these emotional needs in strange ways, but the quest for Love and acceptance is a Universal drive in everyone. I allow it in myself and recognize it in others and this awareness has made Life much more Loving and pleasant for me.

Recovering From A Loss

When we lose a lover, a child or a dream a fundamental base has been pulled out from under us. We gasp and after catching our breath we have to pick ourself up and learn to Be again. In many ways this is to recreate ourSelf within this new situation. Recovering from trauma takes time. If you throw Self back into work, or run to avoid the emotional depths of your soul, burnout is invited. It may take years to catch up. It may take three jobs or two disappointing marriages before burn out.

If we do not feel Life as it is happening to us then we're either living in the past or running into the future. The only moment we have is the present one. Burying hurts or disappointments is to stockpile heavy energy within, and to fertilize the weeds. The heavy emotions, guilt, fear, anger, regret, sorrow, if buried will burn out anyone's inner light.

The Vicious Cycle

Burnout syndrome has a life of its own. Futility, disappointment and guilt provoke personal crises and depression. As emotions are affected, health problems can develop and the futility and guilt are fueled rather than the passion.

There is no situation in which there are not challenges. In dealing with people there are surprises and frustrations. Helping professionals who don't realize that people must learn to help themselves, are setting themself up for four alarm burnout.

Chapter 2:   Questionnaires

This is one of the most important chapters for you. No two people are the same so it is foolish for me to make a series of recommendations for each of the professions and expect them to work for everyone. Who you are at this moment is a result of all your Life experiences, so how you respond to situations is learned behavior that began practically in the womb.

By taking the time to honestly answer the questions and gauge your responses numerically, you will realize the trouble spots in your Life, you'll know where you need to put your energy and which solutions are best for you.

It is important for you to put ego or image aside, and be honest. No one else needs to see your responses and by repeating the questionnaires in a few months you'll know how you are doing.

In many ways Life is a balancing act, these questionnaires let you know which way the wind blows.

Are You Burning Out?

1 no change 2 some change 3 considerable change 4 big change 5 severe change

Let's look at the past year. Allow yourself time to honestly think about these answers and cover both personal and professional aspects of your life. Then assign it a number from 1 to 5.

1. Are you working harder and accomplishing less? ___
2. Do you tire more easily, feeling drained rather than energetic? ___
3. Are people saying you look tired or asking if things are O.K.? ___
4. Have you felt invaded by a sadness you can't explain? ___
5. Are you disenchanted or cynical? ___
6. Are you increasingly irritable, short tempered? Have you felt a need to apologize for your reactions? ___
7. Are you forgetting deadlines, dates, birthdays, appointments? ___
8. Are you too busy to make personal plans, send notes or cards? ___
9. Are you seeing friends and family less often? ___
10. Is joy a rare feeling for you? ___

11. Are you able to laugh about yourself? ___
12. Is your personal life fulfilling? ___
13. Does sex seem more trouble than it's worth? ___
14. Do you have little to say to people? ___

To place yourself on the burnout scale add the total. Remember this is an approximation and don't become alarmed at a high total but pay attention to it. All burnout is reversible, no matter how far along it is. If you score above 36 start being more nurturing to yourself - not tomorrow, today.

The Burnout Scale
0-25 You're doing fine.
26-35 Be aware of yourself and do things that feel good to you.
36-50 There are changes to be made.
51-65 You're burning out.
over 65 Your choices, values and habits are threatening your life. Change or you may lose it all.

Score ___

Knowing Your Job Stress

Never 2=Rarely 3=bothers me sometimes 4=bothers me a lot 5=bothers constantly

Daily deadlines are a part of my
.
3 4 5

work during what should be off
rs.
3 4 5

My co-workers are difficult to
rk with.
3 4 5

I take on more responsibilities
hout letting go of others.
3 4 5

There isn't much variety or
llenge in my job.
3 4 5

I'm often overwhelmed by the
nands of my job.
3 4 5

When I'm under pressure I lose
temper.
3 4 5

Constant interruptions prevent me
m completing things.
3 4 5

My job is always with me. I'm in
onstant state of lunch.
3 2 1

10. I'm torn between being the model
employee, spouse or parent.
1 2 3 4 5

Total your work stress score.

If the score is below 10 you are handling work stress well, or you've created a positive, nurturing environment for yourself.

10-20 Your work is costing you peace of mind and probably wellness. Time to look at your values.

20-30 Think about what you'll be like in three years as a result of this stress? Are you abusing yourself with drugs or alcohol to cope? How much is the stress costing you?

30+ don't ignore the signals. You're headed for four alarm burnout and a physical shutdown. You're tight, angry and today is the day to gather tools and change the situation and yourself!

Score ____

The Values Exercise

This is the most important part of this book.

From the time you were born you've been told what to value by parents, siblings, grandparents, school, religion, television, movies and advertising. You're constantly bombarded with information telling you what to value. Other people's values are shoulds, your own values are wants. If you lose true values, you burn out.

I suggest you photocopy the values exercise and share it with people close to you, to learn their true values for Life, work or home. This exercise can be used for any facet of Life.

To do the Values exercise:

1. Beside the word category, at the top of the page, write the facet of your Life you want to know about. The first time write Life, other times career, home, relationship, sex, vacation or any other category can be examined.

2. Without struggling or straining your brain, fill the left column windows with five things that you value about the category. If your category is Life a value might be happiness, home and so on.

3. Once the left column is complete fill the *how it is* column with four ways this value is expressed in your Life now. If one of your values is Love, in the how it is column write ways Love is expressed in your Life; people and things you Love. Fill the *how it is* column as best you can. If you don't fill in all four windows for each value it's O.K. to leave blanks.

4. Fill in the *how it could be* column with thoughts on the way you would like this value to be expressed in your Life. If your value is Love and you have a name in *how it is*, in *how it could be* put a way you could Love this person more. Relax, let your imagination give you wonderful, ideal ways this value could be in your Life.

5. Cover the first two columns so you can't see them, look at the groups of four in the *how it could be* column and decide which group is most important, write 1 in the window beside this group. 2, beside the second most important category and so on.

Put your energy into your number 1 & 2 *how it could be* groups in the far right column, that energy will fulfill you and enhance your Life.

If we put energy into our top values the energy comes back as fulfillment. Everything is evolving and so are your values, so allow yourSelf to change. If you always honor your true values you will not burn out.

Values Exercise

category _____

values	how it is	how it could be	#

Finding The Hassle Factors

I propose the Hassle Factor as a tiny measure of how well you're doing at keeping Life pleasant.

Lets go through 20 aspects of daily living that are potential sources of hassle. By grading each on a scale of 0-10, first in terms of its importance to you and then in terms of its quality, you come up with a hassle factor. And lo and behold maybe you'll decide to let some of them fly.

1. Fill the Importance column first. Rate the categories in terms of how much you value them. If a stylish home that other people drool over is important to you then rate it a 9 or 10. If you're happy living in a simple little abode rate it a 2. If your *stuff* is constantly needing repair, upkeep, time and money rate the importance repairs and upkeep have in your lifestyle. If coworkers you respect and enjoy are really important to you rate coworkers a 9 or 10. Do the whole importance list, now. The two spaces at the bottom are for you to insert your own hassle categories.

2. Now we look at the quality of this facet of your life. Rate the quality of your home on a scale of 1 to 10. Do the same for the other categories and be honest with yourself. By realizing the discrepancy, you know where to place your energy. How do you feel about the quality of these elements of your Life?

3. To know your hassle index subtract the Quality from the Importance. The higher the number the greater the discrepancy between its value and its reality.

If the quality number exceeds the importance you will get a negative number. Put a - (minus) sign beside it in the third column. This is an area where you've got bonus points. Why is this a nurturing area of your Life? Did you work on it or relax with it? There is a lot to learn from these bonus areas. Think about them.

To gauge your overall hassle index add up the score column subtracting the bonus points from the total.

This is how much you're being hassled. A hassle free Life would score zero.

Categories with the highest hassle factors require attention. What do you want to do about these areas? Jot down ideas to eliminate the hassle factors. Now that you are aware, the hassle factors will be difficult to ignore.

How Hassled Are You?

Category	Importance	Quality	Scale I - Q
Stylish home	_____	_____	_____
Status symbols	_____	_____	_____
Repairs, upkeep	_____	_____	_____
More money	_____	_____	_____
More Power	_____	_____	_____
Appearance	_____	_____	_____
Coworkers	_____	_____	_____
Lover	_____	_____	_____
Sex	_____	_____	_____
Friendship	_____	_____	_____
Medical care	_____	_____	_____
Commuting	_____	_____	_____
Pollution	_____	_____	_____
Vacations	_____	_____	_____
Recreation	_____	_____	_____
Climate	_____	_____	_____
Health	_____	_____	_____
Happiness	_____	_____	_____
_____	_____	_____	_____
_____	_____	_____	_____

TOTAL HASSLE SCORE _____

How Well Rounded Are You?

You may want to photocopy this page so you can do the test again.
Give the following facets of your Life a rating from one to ten.
One being low satisfaction or fulfillment and ten being very fulfilled.

1. Happiness _____   7. Job _____

2. Love _____   8. Money _____

3. Sex _____   9. Emotions _____

4. Relationships _____   10. Communication _____

5. Your Child Self _____   11. Exercise _____

6. Playing _____   12. Time _____

Now transfer your score from each facet to the corresponding section
in the wheel below. Draw a curved line between the spokes that define
each segment and colour in the space.

Your completed index will look something like this. >

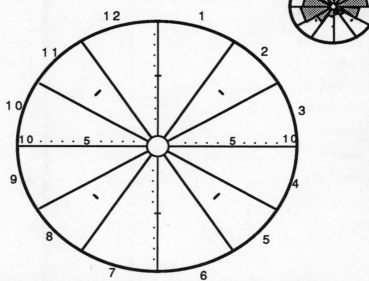

Now that you've completed the wheel, study its shape and balance.
How well rounded is your inner wheel? How smoothly would it
roll? Are there surprises? Where do you need to place your
energy in order to round out your Life?

How Resilient Are You?

0= strongly disagree 1= mildly disagree 2= mildly agree 3= strongly agree

To find out how resilient or hardy you are, answer questions A - L on the blanks in the right column.

A. Doing my best at work makes a difference.

B. An average citizen can have an impact on society.

C. Trusting fate is all I can often do with relationships.

D. Without luck it is hard to succeed in my field.

E. I often wake up eager to start on the day's work.

F. I understand the purpose of what I do at work.

G. Being a free person would be difficult and frustrating.

H. Becoming close to someone means being obligated.

I. If something challenging came along I'd risk financial security.

J. New challenges and situations are important to me.

K. Changing my schedule bothers me.

L. Having nothing to do doesn't bother me.

Add A&B, C&D and subtract the second number from the first. Continue with the three combinations then add control + commitment + challenge for your total resiliency score.

$$\frac{\quad}{A} + \frac{\quad}{B} = \frac{\quad}{}$$
$$-$$
$$\frac{\quad}{C} + \frac{\quad}{D} = \frac{\quad}{} = \frac{\quad}{\text{control}}$$

$$\frac{\quad}{E} + \frac{\quad}{F} = \frac{\quad}{}$$
$$-$$
$$\frac{\quad}{G} + \frac{\quad}{H} = \frac{\quad}{} = \frac{\quad}{\text{commitment}}$$

$$\frac{\quad}{I} + \frac{\quad}{J} = \frac{\quad}{}$$
$$-$$
$$\frac{\quad}{K} + \frac{\quad}{L} = \frac{\quad}{} = \frac{\quad}{\text{challenge}}$$

$$\frac{\quad}{\text{Control}} + \frac{\quad}{\text{Commit}} + \frac{\quad}{\text{Challenge}} = \frac{\quad}{\text{Total}}$$

A total score of 10-18 shows a hardy personality. 0-9: moderate hardiness. Below 0: low resilience.

Score _____

How Are You Coping?

The following questionnaire helps you know how you're coping. Knowledge is not as frightening as ignorance, so whatever you discover is going to make you feel better.

Take some time with each question, remembering instances where you did notice something but dismissed it.

1. Do you feel you are plugging away at something you don't enjoy doing? (relationship, job, family role)

5 4 3 2 1

2. Do you resist discussing your feelings and conflict with your closest friends?

5 4 3 2 1

3. Do you have to force yourself to be considerate or polite to other people.

5 4 3 2 1

4. Are you listless and in search of a diversion?

5 4 3 2 1

5. Would you consistently like to be somewhere else, whether you are at work or at a party?

5 4 3 2 1

6. Is a sexual relationship more of a burden than a pleasure?

5 4 3 2 1

7. Do you have a drink to change or maintain your frame of mind?

5 4 3 2 1

8. Do you use tranquilizers or sleeping pills? Find out what your medications are for if you don't know.

5 4 3 2 1

9. Are you wanting new sexual encounters with new people?

5 4 3 2 1

10. Have you lost control of yourself or been ashamed of your actions in the past year?

5 4 3 2 1

11. Is your temper under control?
5 4 3 2 1
12. Does the future seem bleak?
5 4 3 2 1
13. Have you wanted or looked for pills, cigarettes, drugs, alcohol or promiscuous sex more often in the past six months?
5 4 3 2 1

Score _____

If your total is:
55-65 - You are coping well. Look at the areas where you scored below 3. Keep tabs on these areas.
45-55 - There are signs of pressure, burnout and false cures. The areas where you scored below 3 need change.
35-45 - You're leaning toward dependency on false cures. Are you ready for change? Addiction is a painful threat.
25-35 - You're not coping well. Isn't it time to get help?
less than 25 - You're dependent and this is making it harder for you to cope. Get some help to stop using substances. How bad does it have to get before you'll get better?

Are You A Positive Thinker?
1= never 2= rarely 3= sometimes 4= usually 5= always

1. Do you like most people when you meet them?

1 2 3 4 5

2. If someone is looking at you, is it because they find you attractive?

1 2 3 4 5

3. When you have to change plans, are you quick to spot hidden advantages to the new agenda?

1 2 3 4 5

4. Does your state of mind affect your health positively?

1 2 3 4 5

5. Do you pause to admire beautiful things?

1 2 3 4 5

6. Are you surprised when a friend disappoints you?

1 2 3 4 5

7. Do you believe the human race will survive into the 21st Century.

1 2 3 4 5

8. Do you know the difference between useful criticism and 'sour grapes' which are better off forgotten.

1 2 3 4 5

9. Are you a happy person?

1 2 3 4 5

10. If you're stopped for speeding and you're certain you weren't, would you take it to court?

1 2 3 4 5

11. Are you comfortable being the butt of your own jokes?

1 2 3 4 5

12. Do you think you'll be better off next year?

1 2 3 4 5

13. If you made a list of ten favourite people are you one of them?

1 2 3 4 5

14. Over the past six months which stand out successes or unsuccesses?

1 2 3 4 5

Score _____

60+ a superstar optimist

55-60: a positive thinker

50-55: sometimes positive. Try not to let a mood affect your perception.

45-50: equal positive to negative. Life is only half bad, right? Try seeing the glass as half full rather than half empty. Negativity will make you burnout.

45 and below: Look at your consistent negative patterns. for the next three days find the positive in each situation. Block negative thoughts and think positive ones. See if it is better. Exchange the word but for and.

Stress Rating Scale

Score the events you've experienced in the past year and add the total. If you don't agree with the number assigned, put your own number on the line.

Event	Value	Event	Value
Death of spouse	10___	Trouble with in-laws	2___
Divorce	9___	Outstanding achievement	2___
Death of close family member	8___	Spouse begins or stops work	2___
Marital Separation	7___	Starting or finishing school	2___
Jail Term	7___	Revision of personal habits	2___
Personal Injury or illness	5___	Changed work hours	2___
Getting Married	5___	Change in residence	2___
Fired from work	5___	Change in schools	2___
Retirement	5___	Change in recreation	1___
Marital reconciliation	4___	Change in church	1___
Family member illness	4___	Change in social activities	1___
Pregnancy	4___	Change in sleeping habits	1___
Sex Difficulties	4___	Change in eating habits	1___
Addition to family	4___	Vacation	1___
Change in financial status	4___	Minor violation of the law	1___
Business readjustment	3___		
Trouble with boss	3___		
Death of close friend	3___		
Change line of work	3___		
More marital arguments	3___		
Son or daughter leaving home	2___		
Mortgage or loan over $10,000	3___		
Mortgage or loan foreclosure	3___		
Change in work responsibilities	2___		
Mortgage or loan under $10,000	2___		

Score _____

Add your total. We each respond to situations individually, but it is valuable to know whether you are creating stressful events. Are you burning out because of a stressful year? Some people will sabotage themselves by creating stressful events during an already stressful time. By reducing negative stress we reduce burnout. Decide which stresses are negative and which are positive.

Measuring Yourself On The Burnout Wheel

Knowledge is power, particularly when it applies to your own Life. To see how you are doing, and the areas that need your energy, copy your scores from the eight questionnaires into the spaces labelled raw scores. Get a calculator and do the mathematical adjustments to make each score a percentage. It takes a few minutes but if seeing is believing, the results are worth it.

	Raw score	Equation	Percentage
Positive Thinking	_____	X 1.54	_____
Hassle Index	_____	x .50, subtract result from 200	_____
Well Rounded	_____	X .83	_____
Job Stress	_____	x 2, subtract result from 100	_____
Coping	_____	X 1.54	_____
Burnout Scale	_____	x 1.43, subtract answer from 100	_____
Resilience	_____	X 5.55	_____
Stress Rating	_____	÷ 4.3, subtract answer from 100	_____

To see the areas that need your attention fill in the burnout wheel on the next page the same way you did the well rounded wheel but remember this scale is from zero to one hundred.

Is your inner wheel round.? Are you filling the wheel? The areas that need your attention prevent the inner wheel from rolling. Look at the questionnaires you score poorly on and think of ways you can overcome the challenges.

In a few months, after dealing with the trouble areas and pressure points, do all the tests again and see how you're Beating Burnout.

The Burnout Wheel

Enter your percentages from the previous page onto the spaces below and fill in the burnout wheel the same way you did the well rounded wheel on page 24.

1. How positive   _____
2. Job stress   _____
3. Hassle Index   _____
4. Stress Scale   _____

5. Well Rounded   _____
6. Coping   _____
7. Resilient   _____
8. Burnout   _____

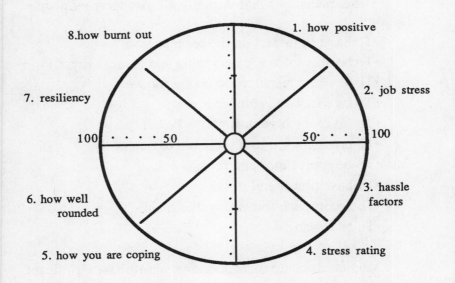

Chapter 3:   Burnout In Management

Researchers Ayala Pines and Elliot Aronson asked managers to list their hopes and expectations when they started their current job. The result, <u>published in their book</u> "Career Burnout Causes and Cures" reveals two main themes - <u>a need for personal independence</u> and <u>freedom and the need to be successful</u> and receive recognition for it.

The expectations that virtually all management people list are:

- •To have an impact on the organization
- •To be able to do my own thing and express myself
- •To have the resources to do the job well
- •To be a success, number one
- •To make the organization the best it can be
- •To prove myself to myself and to others
- •To be appreciated and recognized
- •To have power and status
- •To accomplish something worthwhile
- •To be rewarded

Motivated management personnel want to have significant impact on their organization by doing their own thing, for which they need to have adequate resources. They don't want to just do their job, they want to be exceptional, number one, resulting in the organization excelling because of their personal input.

On a deep level managers expect their success at work to be very fulfilling and to give their life a sense of value.

But reality rarely meets expectation. When managers are asked to list the stressful aspects of their work this is what the lists look like.

- Not enough control to have impact
- Not enough money to accomplish the task
- Staff shortages
- Administrative and bureaucratic hassles
- Not enough recognition and salary
- Not enough room for advancement
- I can't do things the way they should be done

Reality did not meet values or expectations. The idealistic managers discovered the real world of business to be one of shortages, politics, blockages and frustrations.

When the frustration is chronic, when the "I can't get ahead" or "it can't be done under these conditions", attitude is chronic, it leads to a sense of failure. Enthusiasm, commitment and ambition wanes. The challenge becomes humdrum. The bounce goes out of the step. After being stifled and stomped on, expectation sours into a sense of failure. The passion for work is smothered, the fire within is starved of fuel and, since most North American executives egos are plugged into their career performance, Life loses its meaning. The perception among the burnt out is that the corporation has let them down, they feel negative, cynical, and depressed.

Managers are not different from any other work group: when their work experience doesn't match their ideal, they're not achieving their expectations. The result is often Self blame and working harder to realize the dream. This combination is deadly, leaving the management person on a treadmill. They live without a real Life, chasing after an ideal that probably can't exist.

It Isn't The Money

Talented managers do not work hard because of money, even though they like to be well paid. Managers who perform well do so because they expect their work to make their life matter in the larger scale of things. They expect their efforts to give meaning to their existence. They don't need either a "carrot" or a "stick" to motivate them because they've attached their personal sense of self worth to their work.

Do

In a supportive environment, with independence, resources, encouragement and freedom from red tape, these managers can reach peak performance. Their sense of significance and achievement can be nurtured and the original motivation fueled.

Don't

If these same people are thrown into a competitive environment, overloaded with work, stifled by bureaucratic interference, poor communication and the need to justify almost everything, they're trapped below their level of competence. They feel unappreciated, insulted, confused, frustrated and without a sense of meaning.

Study results published in the book "Organizational Stress and Individual Strain" by J.R. French and R.D. Caplain reveal that the more successful a professional feels, the less likely they are to burn out. Those with more frustration and failure are more likely to burn out. But this does not mean that the person who feels successful and motivated can push themselves non-stop without risking burnout. That would be like saying as long as someone enjoys eating and drinking, he or she can eat and drink forever without problems.

Historical Views Of Work

Throughout history work has not been the path to self fulfillment. In Biblical times work was regarded as a punishment God handed down for disobeying him. For the ancient Greeks the word work (ponos) means pain. It wasn't until the Protestant Reformation that people were programmed to derive self worth from work. Before this Life was validation enough.

In simpler times people were closer to the Earth and the elements of Life. There was a faith in a higher, wiser reality. The worship of God and Life has now been replaced by business and "the bottom line".

An addiction to work happens only among people who do not deal with the basics of Life directly, the need for food, clothing and shelter. People more grounded in the realities of Life are not addicted to work, they do not suffer from depressions. The question "Do I work in order to live or do I live in order to work" is not perplexing to people in agriculture.

The time famine is a phenomenon of the 90s. Technology is increasing the heartbeat, while computers process complicated data in a trillionth of a second, we don't have time to catch our breath. We are now inundated with information and the mind can't handle it all. All the work saving devices are actually making us work harder, there aren't as many pauses and the half-life of most job skills is dropping rapidly. This is the burnout decade.

Changes In The Family

The dissolution of the family unit also contributes to the generation of people looking for validation and identity through work. Tragically, as someone allows Life to become more complicated, the family is usually the first institution to fall.

The attitude is, I'll survive without a marriage, but I won't survive without my job.

In the agricultural society of our grandparents an individual's sense of Self worth and identity were clear. A person's role contributions to Life and the well being of loved ones was clear. The emotional support system was more intact and permanent... questioning the purpose of Life or *why am I alive,* was more rare. Those who deal with the Earth, Nature and survival issues do not have as many existential crisis and depressions.

If you've ever said "money makes the world go round" you've bought into this social mentality. You need only speak with a recent graduate of a business school to realize that achievement in the business world is approached with a religious fervor. Self-definition through achievements at work is a primary goal for executives and our society. Yet true fulfillment comes from a combination of Life successes.

Society programs managers to seek "Cosmic significance" through processing information. It is an invisible and untactile environment where the payoffs are measured by images on a screen or numbers on a page, none of which have any real or *natural* qualities. The "sweet spots in time", those moments of fulfillment are temporary and not based on anything very tangible. Real progression and contribution isn't easily measured when the accomplishment is barely visible and is as temporary as a projection on a video screen.

The Torture Of Sisyphus

The myth of Sisyphus tells how as punishment Sisyphus was condemned to push a large rock to the top of a mountain whence the rock would roll down again. The gods had thought that "there is no greater punishment than futile and hopeless labor." Today's technocratic worker spends every day at the same tasks with a daily fate often no less absurd than that of Sisyphus. The absurdity and tragedy is that it only becomes apparent during the rare moments when the worker raises his or her head and becomes conscious. If a change is made, the worker can survive intact, but too often the reality is painful, so the head goes back down and the myth continues for yet another day.

The Power Elite

When an executive rises to the position of Chief Executive Officer our cultural definition of "hero" is met. This kind of power, recognition and money does provide enough fulfillment for a *lucky* few. But this path to heroism is a narrow one. There are few places at the top.

Most who do grasp the ring experience depression or a feeling of being empty because the victory isn't very tangible and comes with a heavy price. It seems that to achieve in business you have to forfeit a Life.

Even for business "heroes" work is not enough to give life meaning indefinitely. Once an expectation is fulfilled and the thrill of victory has subsided...then what?

In a business climate more fickle than anything Nature created, a past success is no guarantee of a future one.

I'm being blunt here. I don't intend to burst the balloon. Anyone who visualizes the future, recalls the past and thinks about the rewards of business will produce the same conclusions.

Childhood and media programming, education and your fantasies may have promised a rose garden, but in reality the garden is weedy, everybody is trying to get in and there are a lot of pricks in the way of the blooms.

The Causes Of Stress

Managerial stress tends to result from three factors: (1) uncertainty of outcome, (2) importance of the results and (3) the lack of control over the outcome.

All three factors hinge on control. In today's business climate profit rests on so many variables that no one has control. No corporation controls the health of the national economy, the availability of raw materials, labor and the development of technology. How much control can a manager realistically feel?

Add to all this the pushes and pulls of producing the quantity for profit while maintaining the quality, and you've got a pressure cooker. And don't forget the younger people after your job, the older people who aren't getting out of your way and the politics of keeping your head above water.

It is a tough, artificial jungle out there and in the concrete towers there is very little shade. It becomes a case of do or die, so people become workaholics, making the career a single, all-involving preoccupation, the only thing in Life that seems to matter because everything else - relationships, home, recreation, life*style*, hinge on the career. The recreation is with clients and business peers, the vacations are "performance perks". Everything is invested in the work, so there is little or nothing left for anything else.

Why Burnout Is A Benefit

Burnout is the way your inner wisdom is telling you you're out of balance, selling your soul, not *doing Life* quite right.

Systems - education systems, corporate systems - do not acknowledge souls, the fact that you are a spirit in a body, that you are a totally unique creation of consciousness. Your education homogenized you by not encouraging an awareness of Self or individuality and it is likely you've allowed your business environment to do the same. Without Self expression the Self is stifled. The essence of you is Self, Soul, Spirit. It is a powerful force that needs care and nurturing. Unless Self is maintained, your robot imitation will become stiff, much like the Tin Man in The Wizard of Oz; without heart we rust and fall apart.

Creating Success

I do not use the word failure because the word is over used and abused. We only fail when we abandon something that we value, when we quit trying to overcome a challenge that is still important to us.

If you are like most people you were programmed as a child with the parental advice "don't start something unless you're going to finish it". We all had parents spend money on music lessons or a musical instrument, dance classes, or a uniform for a sport we didn't play. Parents lay on a guilt trip because "you didn't finish what you started". But how do you finish something like music lessons, how do you finish any artistic or creative endeavor? Where are the finish lines in Life?

There are no finish lines, only personal goals you set. People burn out in situations where the rewards are no longer interesting and the passion has left. This isn't wrong, bad or failure. It is a lesson in living.

A person's spirit may have stopped coming to work years ago, but the body is still there. As I see it, you only have two choices, if you can't Love it leave it; and if you can't leave it change it so you can Love it.

Life is not a dress rehearsal and there is no finish line.

Goals And Passions Are Internal

Success is an absolutely personal achievement. It is Self established, Self motivated and Self accomplished. We really do have to realize and satisfy our own values in Life.

Your feelings of success are absolutely internal. You determine what level of achievement is desirable and possible for you and then go for it. If you have a quota imposed on you, you decide whether it is realistic. Too often a real success is cancelled by outside influences.

Achievements are a personal perception of a reality. For example if a student got 92 percent on an exam we might consider it very successful and so might the student. But if his three best friends got 96 percent on the same exam the student might turn it into a failure. Success must be internal.

You might be successful by your own standards and not know it. You might be denying yourself fulfillment by looking at your neighbor rather than looking at yourself. We only feel weak by comparison.

If you are constantly comparing yourSelf with others, or if your organization sets up a competition, you may be a winner without knowing it. If you are constantly measuring success, not against your own aspirations and needs, but the achievements of others, no level of success will suffice. And this only adds to the pressures that produce burnout.

Obsessions

Achievement is Self destructive when it dominates a person's existence.

Listen to this executive: "I'd immersed myself in my career, working night and day, weekends and holidays to establish my business and make more money. Suddenly I realized I don't know my wife, I don't know my kids and I don't know myself any more. I didn't have a life any more. I thought I'd been relaxing but then I realized that when I played golf it was an extension of my office. I didn't have any real friends because I only socialized with clients and business associates. The conversation revolved around work rather than Life. I realized Life was passing me by... I know what people mean by selling your soul."

The double bind results from the push for achievement and the absence of the real elements of living.

Achievement oriented people are often doomed. Success is often devastating and depressing. Think of the astronaut who has a break down after making it to the moon; of the scientist who falls apart after making the discovery that would and did change his Life, of the actor who works only for the Oscar and loses the pleasure of the craft. The sudden recognition is accompanied by severe depression. The song "Is that all there is" comes to mind. If professional achievement is *all* there is, success is doom. For obsessed achievers, failure is bad enough... but success is even worse.

A life dominated by a future success is geared for that one moment in the sun... and that moment is usually painful because the price of obsession is evident.

Winning With Success

In order for success to be positive rather than painful we must learn to relax and enjoy the small successes along the way and to make those celebrations the "sweet spots in time" that lead to more great moments. We must also learn to appreciate the simple pleasures, the majesty of Nature and

Self expression through music or art. We must learn to care for each other and Love and revel in the wonderfulness of Life. When we do, success in business is in balance, Life is in balance and burnout is averted.

Overwork and 'I'm Indispensable'

It is important to make distinctions between the concrete demands of the job and the demands you place on yourSelf. It is likely you are assuming or blaming your position, your supervisor or organization for demands you've placed on yourSelf. Some people overwork, assuming this is a demand of their job, but an honest look reveals you are the taskmaster, not the job or your supervisor. People who believe long hours lead to success are working hard, not smart.

Many chief executive officers and other "higher ups" surround themselves with people and don't train them to make decisions and handle responsibilities. The person who enjoys power often sets up an ego-gratifying conceit that they are indispensable. They are handling the big decisions and the small ones. They have underlings running to them with questions and fearing punishment from the person who is keeping secrets so others won't have the tools for making good decisions.

By training people, giving them the information and tools to make decisions and delegating authority, any supervisor or director becomes more balanced.

Behaving as though you can't leave the office and

have to do everything yourSelf means you have bad hiring practices or bad delegating skills or both. If your people can't handle things make some changes, start by educating them.

Mid Career Crisis

A mid career crisis can trigger burnout in people who have maintained high ideals, motivation or enthusiasm. It happens to people who've made career choices at an early age. They start out convinced that by being a corporate executive, a doctor or a lawyer, they will make a major contribution to society and they will be loved and accepted.

"What do you mean, what am I doing home?"

By mid career one episode resulting in a sense of failure can bring it all tumbling down. They realize their contribution may be far smaller than they had hoped, or they begin to resent their career because society doesn't deserve the sacrifice they've made. They start feeling empty, disillusioned, painfully aware of their mortality and the passage of time. "Wait a minute. This isn't what I want for the rest of my Life" has been said by many midlife burnouts. They look at the past, the predictable future, and the present and they burn out.

I do not believe we were born to cover this planet in concrete and fast food outlets. I think a midlife burnout is a healthy reaction. It is a cue to step off the treadmill, look at Life and realize true values.

Sometimes the rug has to be pulled out from under us for us to realize society's version of success may not be a soul's version of success.

We need to stop from time to time and evaluate our Self imposed demands and our values to determine whether we're fulfilling ourSelves.

If you ignore that you are an evolving spirit within a body, you are setting yourSelf up for a fall.

Physical Or Emotional

People tend to be physical or emotional types. Most male programming teaches boys to be interested in the physical realities of Life. To play in the dirt, to build, create and possess.

Female programming focuses much more on feelings and emotions. The emotional person's way of living is "I feel therefore I am". The physical's attitude is, "My body is here so I am here". The physical person is validated by the *stuff* of Life and is likely to search for fulfillment through material gain.

When a divorce, death, illness or failure pulls the rug out from under a physical person, they tumble into foreign territory. They're suddenly experiencing their emotional Self. They FEEL Life now and the feelings can hurt. The old blocking mechanisms like sports, working harder, hunting or fishing may salve the hurt for a time but the emotional Self is asking for representation in this Life. The child within who may have been seriously hurting for a long time cries out for Love, nurturing, forgiveness and fun.

If the emotional Self is denied, the person will often sink into a chemical dependence or workaholism until the body responds to the emotional hurt through dis-ease.

The child/emotional self that we all contain will wait patiently to be honored, but if the Self is hurting and neglected it will respond loud and clear. Heart attacks, high blood pressure, cancer and other immune deficiency illnesses are the Self's way of saying "I've stopped pussy footing around, it is time to become conscious of the wonderment of consciousness, it is time to embrace Life".

It is sad so many people forget to appreciate Life until they are facing their exit.

Management Solutions

Corporate burnout results not just from reality not meeting ideals, it is a question of balance. Burnout is not a result of the task, it is in the denial of the Self and true values.

We are human beings with physical and emotional Selves. Both must be honored. A sense of coherence to Life is required in order for Life to flow and function. To beat burnout we need to realize that Life is comprehensible, that one's Life is validated by simply Being, that we live within a very neurotic society and within an un-neurotic higher reality based on Life, energy and Truth. The Self is not manmade it is linked to a Cosmic plan and Cosmic significance is fulfilled through Living, not through working.

Celebrate The Small

Achievement and growth need to be celebrated independently. Celebrating each level of success serves as a powerful buffer against burnout, and it is important for us to acknowledge and bask in our own growth before pushing into the next phase.

Too many ignorant managers will barely notice today's achievement before talking about tomorrow's challenge. Break the torture of Sisyphus, if you've pushed that rock up the hill spend some time with it on the top. Enjoy, celebrate, indulge yourSelf. If you don't relish all the victories, there won't be as many. It is a mistake to let competition subvert our experience of success.

The Comfort Of Change

Since you were born you have been in a constant state of change. Nothing has stayed the same. Nothing will stay the same, no matter how hard you work against Universal laws.

Change is natural and enjoyable. Let me teach you about change. Here is an exercise. Take your hands and clasp them in front of you. Notice which thumb is on top. Now separate your hands and clasp them again, this time with the other thumb on top.

Feels kind of strange doesn't it?

O.K. now unclasp and reclasp the first way. Now unclasp and clasp the new way... the old way the new way. Each time it becomes more comfortable.

This is the essence of change. You'll soon be able to clasp with either thumb on top with equal comfort.   Change is simply stretching your comfort zone as you try something new. You can almost always go back to the original way if you don't like the new way. By allowing yourSelf to try positive new things you'll eliminate the trauma of change and reduce the risk of burnout.

Physical Changes

If you want to avoid burnout a physical plan is needed. I know that if exercise isn't easy and comfortable it won't last, so find exercise you enjoy. Join a great health club, walk up stairs whenever possible, get off one subway stop early, park on the outside edge of the lot.

When you are exercising or walking, quiet your mind, notice the colour of the sky, take a moment to look up and avoid thinking about business. It is impossible to stay angry when we are looking up.

Doing stretching exercises between appointments help pull the tensions out of cramped muscles.

Contrary to what most mothers say, it isn't necessary to clean up your plate. Become a healthy restaurant orderer, eat only what feels comfortable and stop. Skip seconds and stay away from fried foods.

When you are tired what you probably don't need is food, what you do need is physical activity to get some fresh energy. Ask your inner wisdom "what do I need now?".

Coffee intake needs to be limited. It is probable you're taking in exactly what you don't need when you get a coffee. Coffee increases tensions and stress. Juice is better and hot water with a spoonful of honey is also good. If that sounds sissy, remember, it is the bullies that burn out.

Do Lunch Well
Here are the five commandments for lunch:

Take a full lunch hour.

Take time and enjoy.

Order light, healthy food.

Talk about anything but business.

Stay away from alcohol.

When these commandments are followed lunch is a relaxing, pleasant and stress-reducing event.

If you suspect that three drinks at lunch is expected, excuse yourself from the table, inform the bartender or service person, order like everyone else and get a clean refreshing beverage, not a depressant.

People who claim drinking at lunch doesn't affect their performance, wellness and attitudes are lying to themselves. Alcohol abuse is a false cure, a negative coping mechanism that leads straight into burnout.

It is good to grab some rest during hectic days. Take a catnap, listen to a relaxation tape, close your eyes and fantasize. John F. Kennedy did it and most American Presidents since have taken an afternoon nap. If the presidents can do it we can too.

Values and Goals

By doing the questionnaires and paying attention to the values exercise you'll show yourSelf the places to put your energy. The well rounded wheel is also a way of seeing where you need to channel energy.

Looking at photos of your Self as a child lets you know how you're doing with that nice little kid. Are you taking care of that child? Some people beating burnout have a childhood picture of themself on their desk. What a great basis to make decisions by.

Set Goals & Stop Worrying

By establishing goals that meet both professional and personal expectations you align the facets of your Life. IT can be helpful to keep your values list handy, even on your desk so you can make decisions based on true values.

Executives can be great worriers, a useless practice. By reducing worry time you reduce stress.

Here is a way to stop worrying.

Think of something you are worried about.

Realize the only moment you control is the present one.

What can you do to solve or eliminate the challenge <u>NOW</u>? How can you solve it NOW?

If the time for action or solving isn't now the worry can be released with the knowledge you have an agenda and when it is time to deal with it, when it is a real issue or when the information is available to base a decision on, it can be dealt with, just as you've dealt with everything else. Worrying never helped and it doesn't work.

It is helpful to plan some enjoyable tasks each day and think of ways to delegate tasks you don't enjoy. It is very possible someone else has the skills to enjoy doing that job more efficiently.

It is by doing the enjoyable that intellectual burnout is avoided.

You Generate All Your Feelings

This is an important step in realizing the control and response - ability you have. You live within your mind and no one else can take control of that. Irrational beliefs like "I must succeed" or "I must be liked by everyone" are killers. How can someone like you if they don't like themSelf? If you've been a good, caring, loving and positive person and they don't accept you, it is their problem not your's.

Dealing With Group Burnout

If there is group burnout in an organization it is time to do something about it. A few copies of this book, an emotional health program and burnout seminar or counselling are in order. The time invested in helping people, pays off in a multitude of ways. According to Dr. Peter Hanson author of "Joy Of Stress" and "Stress For Success" for every dollar invested in wellness the return is as much as five dollars.

Seeking Balance

Most emotional stress comes from imbalance. Find out how well rounded you are and know where your energy is required. Don't give guilt any room in your mind. Take care of yourSelf. Burnouts aren't much good to anyone.

When surprises or disappointments arise take a long breath and think the words "I choose peace". That moment of maintaining control gives your creative subconscious - your inner wisdom, a moment to formulate a positive and healthy reaction - which is often no reaction at all.

Read the section on decompression after work, it is vital for business people.

Insist On Happy Hellos

A happy greeting is possible in any situation, it lets the person know you see them and value them.

Insist on fifteen positive minutes on arriving home. There is nothing worse than coming home to complaints and problems from a spouse and children. The *wait till your father gets home* approach is destructive to all the family relationships.

Family is often eager to dump their problems on you when in fact they need to develop their own Life skills. Establish that no one be greeted with a problem. After a few positive moments together the challenges of the day can be dealt with much better.

The Value Of A Shoulder

It is vital to have a confidant. This can be a friend or it can be a paid professional. You are not alone in your feelings and responses to the insane situations created by this increasingly complicated society. Burning out is not a weak reaction, it is an honest reaction.

Make a deal with yourSelf. Whatever the pressures of the job don't let them interfere with your friendships. Spend time with people you like at least once every two weeks.

If busy executives would spend 30 minutes each day with children the unreal pressures and expectations of the job become very incidental. Children are born very good at Life. They are in touch with their wants, feelings, likes and dislikes and they're not ashamed to get what they need for themselves. Socialization can be a process of losing touch with true needs.

Everyone carries the child within. If we appeal to and nurture the Child Self in ourSelf and in others we will be valued and respected for our insights and wisdom.

Vary Vacations

Vacations can be scenic, educational, romantic or nonsensical. Some vacations are for the mind, some for the body and some for the soul. There are vacations for kids and vacations for adults. We need them all. When planning a vacation, ask your inner wisdom what you need and for how long and have your travelling companion(s) do the same.

Two people on the same vacation for different reasons need to know what they need and find it independently.

Stay Grounded

People in large urban centres who live and work in towers have scattered energy. I am sensitive to people's auras and know whether they are grounded. We are products of the Earth. We were not designed to be tree dwellers. We need contact with the Earth. When you are feeling scattered go out and sit at the base of a tree, sit on the ground. We know enough to ground our refrigerators, our stoves and dishwashers but we forget to ground ourselves.

The planet is our mother.

Decruitment

Some fast-lane veterans who are fed up with their harried existence are trying innovative escape routes, including climbing down the corporate ladder. They're trading in the big salary for a lower-level job that offers more vacation time, flexible hours, longer maternity or paternity leave and evenings and weekends off. They're taking their Life back with decruitment.

Surprisingly many managers are snapping up the opportunity to do some hands-on work again. They take the less prestigious jobs, some saying they want their children to know them as something besides their provider.

Many companies now interview all managers at age fifty-five to see if they want early retirement or decruitment. Those who have "decruited" say it was a wise choice.

You Will Never Be A Machine

You can't keep your nose to the grindstone all the time. When you do, you can't see what is in front of your face.

There are many choices and opportunities for creativity. There are many types of success and many people discover true success by relaxing and having fun. Take your time going through the solutions chapters. It isn't a race to get finished, it is a time to think, reflect and embrace changes.

Thinking about the type of person you would like to be, realizing the burnout factors in your Life, your true values, embracing change and the tools for Loving and nurturing your Self is what this book is about.

Chapter 4: Burnout in Bureaucracies

One-third of our waking lives is spent working, often in environments that totally ignore human needs, emotions and potentials. It is only since the mid 1970s that concern for people in the workplace has become widespread, but humanization has a long way to go. We only need to look at the number of offices with windows that don't open, the number of work spaces lit by fluorescent lights, and the number of training programs that don't equip people for surviving the job, to realize we've got a lot to remember about Being.

There is a growing awareness of the disfunctional aspects of mega corporations and cities. In the 90s the high draw cities are not the metropolises of New York, Los Angeles or Toronto, the fast growth centers are smaller, more human climes of Albuquerque, Fort Worth, Providence, Victoria B.C. or London, Ontario. To many working families a higher quality of Life compensates nicely for the absence of live opera and slick entertainment options.

Major corporations are finding their brightest people are experiencing early signs of burnout, packing up the family and moving to a smaller town where Life is on a human scale. Corporations have major dollars invested in these people, expecting them to remain for the long haul. But increasingly people in tune with their stress levels, wants and values say farewell to the corporation as through it is a graduate school. They're moving out on their own to set up small consulting firms or join a *humanized* organization. The humanization of America is a mega-trend.

Those who stay with the big organization are often the walking wounded, unable to haul themselves up because they've drifted too far into the long haul.

Society's Burnout

The trend away from the urban centre is a reflection of the burnout of our large cities and our society in general.

People working in complex bureaucratic organizations walk out into a city increasingly congested, unresponsive and oblivious to the human needs of the individual. Their lives are no longer on a human scale. For the person ragged from things moving too fast or too slow, tranquility may not seem possible, but with creativity and awareness it is.

The Humanization of America is a quiet, easy response to the lack of humanity, ease and common sense in our bureaucratic societies.

Climbing Down Off The Dinosaur's Back

Often the bureaucracy is now solving the issues that needed solutions two years ago. They are often self serving rather than public serving and riding on the back of one of these dinosaurs can be frustrating, demoralizing and dehumanizing.

Identifying the "boss" can be like chasing fleas on a St. Bernard. You're never sure if the one you've got is the one you were looking for.

This unclear responsibility results in an inability to get the answer or correct a grievance. People within the organization encounter so many levels of supervisors... who are linked with administrators... who are out of touch with the front line issues of the workers... who are *doing* the job seven levels below. The complexity of bureaucracy is also a popular scapegoat. The maze is so complicated that passing the buck often seems to work, but of course nothing is resolved and this contributes to everyone's burnout.

Workers are often bewildered about how to do the job. There may be a constant flow of new programs with new regulations and policies created by people who are several levels away from those most affected by the policy. By the time one policy is understood and implemented another keen administrator has a replacement coming down the pike.

Because communication skills aren't emphasized in business training, some instructions can be vague to the point of being ineffective while others are explained in such minute detail the intent is muddled.

Unless communication is simplified to convey the message clearly and without jargon and egos clouding the message, burnout is a strong possibility. Most people in bureaucracies are nothing more than information handlers. Their product is paper and too often the paperwork is not simple, clear and concise. This takes its toll on a daily basis.

Paper is only two dimensional and so is the fulfillment that can be derived from it. We need to see real results; how our contribution is benefitting someone and often this has to be Self generated.

Moving Through The Maze

The promotion system within bureaucracies is often a source of burnout because promotions are based more on seniority, ease of movement, convenience, personality or political decisions rather than as acknowledgement for special effort, superior performance or ability to do the job.

In the bureaucracy it is possible to burn out and coast for long periods of time, spreading burnout through a staff. Without drive or passion coming from the leader the others quickly lose any passion, and either settle in among the ashes of the burnt out department or quit when they realize they can't handle the lack of fulfillment.

Those who settle in, hating Mondays and knowing exactly how many months to retirement, are the walking wounded. They've burnt out but they haven't found the gumption to get out of the situation. Being in the job may seem all right, but as children we have ideas of how it will be, and while it never is as we thought it would be, fulfillment is essential to wellness. To get in touch with that child's values try taking out the old photos and look at who you were then. Remember what you wanted for yourSelf and know you still contain that child.

The walking wounded are destructive and dangerous. They may think their lack of professional fulfillment isn't important, because they haven't made the association between their coping mechanisms - drugs, tranquilizers, cigarettes, alcohol, destructive behaviors, and the prison they call a job.

The walking wounded are a serious problem. The experience is traumatic for the individual, the organization suffers, society suffers and the pent up frustration leads to self abuse, spouse abuse or child abuse.

In many cases the bureaucratic experience doesn't break the human, it tranquilizes and stuns the person into someone seeming to have had a frontal lobodomy.

Passion is either driving or consuming. Driving passion leads to achievement. Unexpressed passion consumes, it short circuits with nervous, emotional or physical disorders. The body is talking but the inhabitant isn't listening, and the result is too often tragic.

Life is not a dress rehearsal.

The Good Bureaucrat

Training programs rarely teach students how to be good bureaucrats. People working in bureaucracies are generally unprepared for dealing with the types of stress these organizations generate. This is particularly true for people who work in human services where they find themselves being a clerk, handling stacks of forms rather than working with people.

Work for most people is central to Life, this unfortunately is the North American social psyche, yet the bureaucracy does not honor the individual's need for attaining fulfillment through work.

Bureaucracies tend to burn people out in three ways: [1] overload without consideration for the person, [2] lack of input and independence and [3] lack of rewards. All three are a failure on the part of the organization to take care of people first and paper second.

Overload

Bureaucratic workers generally are inundated with information, be it phone calls, letters, memos, office visits or planning meetings. The mind can't handle it all. The pace can be so fast an office worker may feel like a gunfighter dodging bullets. The pace of a society in which supercomputers operate in a trillionth of a second and the information explosion leaves professionals swamped and reeling from the constant impact. Workers are finding it takes all their energy just to remain qualified for their jobs. There is no question the half-life of most job skills is dropping all the time. The irony is that all the time saving devices are actually making people work harder.

Mount the effects of overload with a feeling of having too much work to do, magnify it with a sense of lack of support and compassion either from above or below and the stage is set for four alarm burnout.

Overload comes in two forms, information overload. Telephone calls, letters to read and write, office visits, meetings, conferences, books all require time and energy. Notoriously bad communicators can survive within a bureaucracy, but the people they're communicating to suffer because of vagueness or confusion. Often the volume of memos is honored over the information in any of them.

One would think that the vast volume of information bureaucrats see would contain the knowledge and skills required to stay on top of the job, but this isn't the case. Most of the information bureaucrats deal with does not empower them in their job. Most is a waste of time.

There is a selectivity process that needs to be adopted. Try choosing the information that empowers you in the job and the career and let the other information slide by.

It is not uncommon to hear social workers, police officers or probation officers say their stress comes, not as much from the contact with people as from writing a report in six copies they feel no one will ever read.

Studies indicate a direct relationship between excessive paperwork, red tape and burnout. The more paperwork and red tape, the more burnout. A study of police officers revealed not crime but paper work as their major problem.

The reason overload causes burnout is that it guarantees the sense of failure. If a person meets the demand for quantity they can't meet the demand for quality. If they take the time needed to do the job properly they fail requirements for quantity. This is devastating for people who care about their work and for whom work equals Self worth.

Dealing With Overload

Overload is a double edged sword because it cuts down the time we have to do the job and hacks away at our authority to make decisions and get things done.

Overload contributes to mental and physical stress levels and rains on your parade.

In a complex bureaucracy overload is guaranteed. During the first six months of a new job overload is at its highest. We're expected to process so much knowledge and so many rules that the mind becomes boggled. In most organizations training is inadequate and the "new kid on the block" is left to figure it out on their own.

The "new kid" is overloaded and feeling inadequate, out of place, alien and guilty and for some employees these first impressions never leave. By thinking or saying things like "I'm not cut out for this", or "I'll never be able to do this as well as..." you're setting yourSelf up for burnout. Remember the subconscious mind is always listening and what you say to and about your Self is your truth and reality.

GI GO - Good information in results in good information out. It is vital to always say positive things about yourSelf and you'll get positive things back.

Adequate training for employees is needed to eliminate the initial overload, but that probably isn't going to happen, so here are some ideas for eliminating overload.

-pick and choose what information empowers you and what information is gobbledygook.

-ask peers what is important and what isn't.

-avoid the negative or jaded mandarins, they'll lead you down the path of burnout. You don't need a pity partner, seek out a positive and caring person. Hang out with winners and you're more likely to be one.

- ask the competent person what you need to know, or what they remember about a topic. This can save hours of reading poorly written jargony material designed to boost someone else's ego more than to inform.

-at the first sign of overload make a priority list based on feelings.

-make communications simple and direct. People will understand and may become better communicators as a result.

- write down early impressions of an organization. First impressions are often right. A beginner is not in a position to make changes or suggestions but once you're a part of the operation positive suggestions will be listened to. The inefficiencies you see coming in may be very valid but employees who've been there a while don't see how things can be done differently.

- positive statements result in positive actions. "This could be even better if... " " there could be an improvement by...". As soon as you say a negative people become defensive and stop listening.

- Overload is a fact of bureaucratic life. Feelings of inadequacy, worry, strain or anger are evidence of too much pressure, too heavy a schedule. It is always best to choose the relaxation response. Stop, think about the best actions and get the job done knowing there is never enough time to do everything asked of you. Most human agendas are inhuman so do what is most important to you and your bottom line.

Avoiding Overload

Becoming a good bureaucrat requires knowledge and experience, but the training programs rarely give people the skills. For many the phrase "good Bureaucrat" is a contradiction in terms. In our society the term bureaucrat means inhuman.

The role of bureaucrat has been ignored by educators, writers and researchers yet there is no doubt that achieving one's professional goals in a mega organization requires competence and finesse. Here are skills identified by R. Pruger in "The Good Bureaucrat".

Lack Of Input

Lack of control over our environment is highly stressful, resulting in feelings of helplessness and depression.

We know that people can stand more pain when they control its duration and intensity. Taking control away from the person causes their tolerance to drop dramatically. We also know that the mortality rate in retirement homes is higher among those who did not want to go into the home than with those who made the choice themselves.

The need for control is so great that people will leap forward to accept blame for an accident or boo boo so that they can maintain their sense of value and control. The underlying thinking is: "If it can go wrong then I have impact on it not happening again. Therefore I am important and I do have some control."

Burnout increases as the sense of autonomy, sense of control and discretionary abilities decrease. The lack of voice in decisions that affect one's job, unnecessary rules, and changes without advance notice, are major frustration factors.

The lack of personal control is more apparent and stressful in the lower ranks of an organization. Employees experience a loss of individuality, "like being an insignificant and replaceable part in a gigantic machine". The communication gap between the 'front line workers' and those at the top are often caused by ego. The person at the top forgets he or she is supported by the bottom.

Bureaucracies are usually inefficient distributors of rewards and recognition. This adds to demoralization and burnout. Labor difficulties and strikes can be evidence of group burnout that has not been dealt with in time.

"So we have three in favour, two against...and one casualty."

The Value of Rewards

In some bureaucratic organizations employees are able to withstand great work stress when they are acknowledged and rewarded for work well done. Appreciation on the job is rated as more important than dollars for most people.

Doctors, for example, are as likely to complain about financial strain as secretaries or clerks. In this material society, it seems the *stuff* escalates with the pay and there is never enough money. But the people who felt more appreciated, satisfied and significant in their work are more likely to be content with their income no matter how low it is.

Burnout is more linked to feelings of lack of success, to poor health and lack of self actualization than to salary.

Burnout happens when people feel they are working, in excess of normal requirements and yet their efforts are not appreciated.

One employee says it clearly:"You never get a pat on the back from management no matter how hard you work . The only thing I'll see is a memo when something goes wrong."

Lack of recognition, input and respect are the major factors in burnout within bureaucratic organizations because it deprives people of their Self worth and Self respect. If they can't feel proud of who they are at work, they won't survive.

Bureaucracies can only benefit from providing positive feedback to their employees. As Leo Buscaglia says, "It costs nothing to be nice."

Bureaucratic Solutions

Remember Your Original Goals

You can get caught up in other people's agendas and lose your own. Try doing the values exercise with career as the heading. It really helps to know your top three career values and to keep them nearby, also write down your original goals, the original reason you were attracted to this profession. Put these values and goals on your desk to know why you are there and if you're undecided about the next move look at the values and goals and measure the next move against them. Honor your values and goals and you'll stay in line with wants. At times you'll have to deviate and do something political because it is "of the highest good". When you have to deviate to satisfy someone else's agenda, do it knowing it contributes to your goals, if it doesn't, do whatever you can to get out of it. It is vital to stay in line with your own values and wants.

When offered a new position, no matter how much money is involved, check the new work with your values and goals. It may meet goals for more money but if your top values are dealing with clients, hands on helping, and being out in the field, and you're offered a job in an office locked away from new people, you're walking into burnout. Many people give up their values, goals and passions for an extra five thousand dollars a year. Burning out isn't worth it.

When Something Is Right

Change happens slowly in bureaucracies. The process of decision and action develop at a measured pace. It's challenging to maintain your vitality and enthusiasm when progress is imperceptible.

Being in a bureaucracy means certain comforts and securities, it also means giving up aspects of independence and control.

When people are aware of a problem and ready to take responsibility, the first changes need to be made with the Self. The work situation needs to be seen from a perspective of calm, knowing, strength. Anger and frustration are not positions of influence. The burnt out bureaucrat can't easily discriminate things that can be changes from the things that can't. In fact most burnouts believe everything can be changed if they would only be given the chance. They end up banging their head against stone walls. The assumption that everything destructive and dehumanizing can be changed leads straight into burnout.

Some aspects of bureaucracy simply *cannot* be changed. Bigness results in feelings of individual smallness. After trying to change things without success the smouldering bureaucrat feels hopeless, helpless and may decide nothing can be changed. They then become cynical and simply put in their time.

It is never so hopeless, some negative aspects of organizations can easily be changed. You may have assumed your organization expects and demands things you have placed on yourSelf. Thinking you have to be witty and charming at boring social functions is a burden you've placed on yourSelf. You may be overworking assuming this is a demand coming from your organization when it's a pressure you've placed on yourSelf. You're probably a much harsher taskmaster than your employer and you do have tremendous control over the situation and how you respond to it, so exercise your control.

Success results from a position of strength, awareness and clear thinking, it comes from knowing when to change your thinking and when to change the people and things in your environment.

To the astute bureaucrat things are always more flexible than they seem at first glance. The motivated person plays a game in which positive change is the prize. Bureaucratic job descriptions are often vague. The rules, the schedules the interpretations are usually a bit slippery and can be interpreted to your advantage. This slipperyness requires discretion but the bigness of an organization offers the skillful bureaucrat the majority of control over the job. It is likely you are more in control than you think.

Rather than reacting, try responding. It is more creative. Instead of looking for guidance in the piles of rules and regulations success may blossom after looking for guidance from your own inner wisdom. Bouncing some ideas off of other people and being creative about your work often changes a situation dramatically.

Time and again people hunger for appreciation. While they feel unappreciated they almost never reach out to show appreciation of someone else's work. If you want people to pay attention to your work, acknowledge the good work of others. People may be surprised at first but it feels good and appreciation mushrooms and spreads. Peer appreciation is easy and fun to start and it reduces the need for approval from above, which is sometimes difficult to institute. If the supervisor isn't being appreciated he or she may not appreciate others.

Burnout results from lack of control and feelings of helplessness. No one is helpless. If you accept nothing can be done you've joined the "dead wood", the "paper pushers", the "yes persons" or the "bureaucrats" in the colloquial meaning of the word.

If you supervise other people and believe "nothing can be done...these are the rules" you're not only burning out yourSelf, you're burning out people around you. You're discouraging yourSelf and other people, eliminating spontaneity, creative interpretation of a situation and the possibility of finding a new solution. If you suppress individual expression you are spreading humiliation, negativity, pain and burnout. A manager's tactics of discouraging original thought and enthusiasm is usually motivated by the manager's need to insure that subordinates will burn out, thus justifying his or her own burnout.

Remember, the essence of managing people is to give them what they need to be excellent at what they do.

New employees have fresh insights, enthusiasm and other experiences to build upon. They are usually overly optimistic about the possibilities of change and fulfillment. These people often have tremendous things to offer that would benefit and spark everyone in the division, but instead these bright lights are humiliated, "cut down to size" and dumped on with the same anger, frustration and despair that is the cancer of the rest of the organization.

Looking For The Child Within

If you're working with a jaded mandarin, a robot bureaucrat, one way to find their humanity is by thinking about them when they're asleep at night. Who are they then and what challenges do they have to overcome? Also think about them as a child, full of hopes and dreams and excited about Life experiences. Walking an imaginary mile in their shoes gives a truthful perspective.

Life hasn't turned out the way they expected it to. It doesn't turn out that way for anybody and one of the reasons they're so cold and impersonal is that they're hurting. Forgiveness is a virtue offered to us by Life, if only we could forgive ourselves and each other. Mark Twain expressed it so well when he wrote: "Forgiveness is the fragrance the violet sheds on the heel that has crushed it." An image to keep in mind when you work with others.

As Gandhi taught us, "Hate the sin, love the sinner". Humanity responds to humanity. By being caring and nurturing we invite others to be more human with us. By forgetting the job dynamic, the positions and the labels and all the dehumanizing stuff and going for the child within that person you humanize what are already human interactions. Ask that person good questions, questions that show you care. Since I've learned this lesson I have experienced success wherever I want to go.

When we approach a "cold fish" in a feeling manner the cold one is often shocked, they've bought into the stupid idea that business is no place for emotions or feelings. They may not allow themself to feel, they may retreat, particularly the first time we approach them with human feelings. Remember, there is a hurt child inside. Continue to show this person you are conscious of their feelings and are open to communication. Gradually they will open. There is a big difference between "sucking up" to a person and complimenting their humanity.

In most cases the blocked person will become a supporter. They will try to help you because you've been honest. They have an understanding of who you are because you took the trouble to find out who they are. If they've been hurt many many times they may choose to be totally miserable and nasty, remember we're all doing the best with what we have to work with. People are the way they are because of the experiences they've had.

As my friend Dr. Wayne Dyer teaches, "When you judge another person you do not define him or her, you define yourself as someone who needs to judge."

When you choose to Love and forgive someone else you define yourSelf as someone who loves being loved.

The Child Within You

It is important to think of that child-Self within you. You can do this most easily by looking at pictures of yourself as a child and noticing what the face in those pictures has to say to you.

Who you were as a child was probably purer, more in touch with wants and needs and more forgiving and Self loving. You can learn a lot from who you used to be.

If you've forfeited your values and goals get them in line by accessing that child-Self.

Jaded, unhappy people forget to Love themselves and care for their child-self and they fear change. They're filled with fear, pain and misery. They spread it around and they're always happy to share pain. Don't do it! Stay optimistic and up. People do not want to hear what you are against, they want to hear what you are for. So BE what you are for.

When someone else is negative don't criticize them, they've had that done before. Ask them the good questions you would ask yourSelf. Questions like "how does this behavior work for you", "Does being this way give you what you really want?"

The essence of managing people is to give them what they need to be excellent at what they do. The same goes for managing your Self.

You can assist, motivate, praise and inspire all the people in your Life, regardless of their position in relation to yours. You only need to accept the possibility and then Be it.

Something Can Always Be Done

Although it may not seem it, the people you work with are human. They have feelings, thoughts and human emotions in spite of the fact nobody may have witnessed anything remotely human in the past five years.

Bureaucracies are cold, unfeeling things. Bureaucracies do not breathe, they do not have consciousness, hopes or fears. The people within the offices are the Life and breath. Bureaucracies create books of rules, they limit, define and suck the Life out of everything. The process of organizing stifles originality, creativity, individualism and change.

All change begins with thought. By changing your perception you change your reality.

If You Were The Boss

This requires some real honesty. It is an important exercise that requires honesty with Self.

Think about how you would run an organization. You're at the top with a lot of control. Visualize how you would look, feel and act and how you would organize things.

Now think about that organization five years after you created it. You're successful and influential, enjoying your control, freedom and fulfillment. How are you acting then? Are you making an effort to allow the "little people" to become creative, spontaneous, free thinking and big like you, or do you protect your position as "leader"?

Do you allow individuals to improve their own situation

when it doesn't improve the situation of the organization?

Are there any unhappy or burnt out employees in your organization?

What is their problem?

How do you feel about that employee?

It is quite likely your organization would have problems, communication breakdowns and some frustrated and unhappy employees. It is quite likely you would use authority to maintain the order of things rather than to allow someone else to personally grow.

Organizing anything means setting up a situation in which some people may feel unfulfilled. Think about teams, clubs or group projects you've been a part of. Was there ever an occasion when someone's nose was out of joint or when you had to step on someone's toes? Was there an occasion when someone else stepped on your toes? People who get their toes stepped on a lot are doing too much standing and not enough walking.

Any organization needs some chiefs and some indians. To be a chief and stay there, you simply need to act like one, to think like one and you will be one. Staying a chief means taking care of your tribe, ruling with Love rather than a club or fear. How have you been at that?

What Kind Of Manager Have You Been?

Try answering these questions.

Do you regard any employee as a subordinate?

Are you friendly with people only at your level of achievement or above?

Have you ever not listened to another person's suggestions on how you might be a better person or a better employee?

If you've answered yes to any of these questions you are not giving what you expect from others. So often we expect supervisors to be caring, motivating and nurturing when we are far from it ourselves. Try being the way you expect other people to be and see what happens.

It is easier to complain and point the finger at other people or a big, dead organization than to change your perspective or your Self.

When you do good, good comes back to you.

The True Source Of Fulfillment

Too many managers abuse their subordinates and look for rewards from above. The greatest rewards come from those who work <u>with</u> you. If you choose to nurture, teach, motivate and praise people, you are empowered, you become a true manager. If you can help people to enjoy their work you will experience great recognition.

Being a supportive manager who gives people what they need to be excellent, offers rewards on a higher level. You become a great teacher who uses a divine gift, you choose Love.

You can make anyone feel good about themself, and about their work with a few simple words of encouragement and praise.

The most successful managers do not rule with fear, they care for people. The organization you are a part of is not as important as its people. Take care of your people and business takes care of itself.

Think about it, who do you perform better for, the tyrant who only criticizes or the person who smiles, encourages you, shares wisdom and truly believes you will succeed?

If you believe in the worth of your enterprise, if you show the people involved that you have faith in their abilities, they will excel and everyone will succeed.

This sets up a win/win situation. There may be times when a firm stance is required but achievement needs to be rewarded with praise and celebration. The achiever needs to feel satisfaction, to desire it. Too often a manager says "You did well today but what are you going to do tomorrow?" This is an insidious aspect of sales. You've just pushed a rock up the side of a mountain and the person who supervises you points to tomorrow's rock and mountain rather than celebrating today's. There is no better way to burn out than to deny yourself satisfaction and fulfillment. To wallow, revel and celebrate in accomplishment is necessary to continue accomplishing.

Love

Tell me a better way to eliminate burnout in any organization. The humanization of America rests on the people within our giant corporations, within our governments, within your office, rediscovering that Love is the ultimate positive force.

You will bend over backward for a person who truly cares for and Loves you. Remember that school teacher who allowed you to feel your specialness, remember the people who took the time to know you and share wisdom and Love?

Anyone can be an inspiration if they'll see and nurture the potentials of other people. In a bureaucracy human fulfillment isn't handed down from above, gold watches are. In a bureaucracy fulfillment comes from being a human, caring, real person wherever you are.

Every human being is after the same things, to be Loved and accepted.

All positive change begins with one individual who moves from fear to Love.

Take A Trip To Oz

Remember the The Wizard Of Oz? Dorothy, Toto and the gang are in the Emerald city in which everything has to be green [the colour of money] and the citizens are all rushing around not knowing where they are going. This city - in the movie the skyline of Manhattan was used to represent Oz - was controlled by the Wizard, a mysterious presence ensconced in a large official looking building.

The Wizard ruled the land with bigness, smoke, fire and fear. Everyone was afraid of the Wizard and nobody could really explain why he was a Wizard or what was so wonderful about him, he just was the wonderful Wizard of Oz!

The inner chamber of the Wizard was a very corporate looking space designed, like most corporate spaces, to intimidate us, and the Wizard appeared as a fire breathing, smoke spewing combination of pyro-technics and video projection.

It took the common senses of Toto to pull back the curtain in the corner and expose the short, round, bald little man who was pulling the levers and pushing the buttons to create the monstrous Wizard.

In this wonderful story the Wicked Witch of the West has an army of mindless monkeys who swoop down and carry off whatever she wants. At the time the book was first published the author was criticized for being unAmerican. The good witch who honored the Self and feelings was of the East, the wicked witch who ruled with fear was of the West.

The Wizard of Oz is a wonderful story of a young person who dreams of a perfectly lovely place somewhere over the rainbow. In her dreams Dorothy travels the yellow brick road [yellow being the colour of fear]. She befriends her heart, her mind and her courage and together they conquer greed, evil and the Wizard.

It is a wonderful story in which every element is representational of Life. If you rent or buy the video you'll learn something about yourSelf and the Wizards of our Oz.

At the end of the story Dorothy has discovered that "home" is within her and to live in the shadow of any fearful wizard is to lose the safety of "home".

The management and solutions chapters can help you realize more ways you can beat burnout.

Chapter 5: Burnout Among Caregivers

Caregivers deal with emotional, physical and social pain day after day. They are expected to be skilled and personally concerned in demanding situations over long periods of time.

Caregivers are at the highest risk of burnout of any professional group because they perform emotionally taxing work, share certain personality characteristics that make them vulnerable, and they work in a giving, providing capacity.

People who are sick, in a crisis, or being presented one of Life's *lessons* are often difficult, draining and afraid. The situations are intensely emotional. Dealing with anger, fear, despair, guilt, pain and hopelessness results in the caregiver, without the proper perspectives and tools, absorbing other people's emotions and carrying them home at night.

As I've said to thousands of people in my speeches and seminars, emotions are real things and we can absorb other people's emotional baggage. The heavy emotions are like an anchor chained to your mind, your heart and spirit. Other people's anger and fear are easy to absorb and easy to let go of with the right tools.

I'm now researching and lecturing about messiah complexes. If we don't have wellness, if we aren't taking care of ourselves, can we teach and help others to heal?

My early research indicates we cannot give what we do not have. *Why good people burn out* is a fascinating area that my next book is covering.

Caregiver Stress Points

Specific occupations under the caregiving umbrella have unique stresses.

For the social worker, exposure to family violence coupled with laws that restrict the ability to remove people from destructive homes is haunting.

Nurses who work in children's leukemia wards experience great emotional stress and often carry the pain of their young patients. They feel helpless against inevitable deaths of innocent children.

The teacher of a retarded child may make headway, then see months of work erased by an epileptic seizure.

When we work with people, we're exposed to pain fear and situations that are unexplainable. We see people in painful situations banging their heads against a wall. The caregiver can offer them a solution by leading them to the door and showing them how to walk through. Often the client walks right back to the wall and bang...bang...bang.

The pain has to get bad enough before people will change.

The Caregiver Psyche

Usually those who choose to work in a helping profession are emotional, sensitive and have experienced disappointment. We tend to have great empathy to the suffering of others. In many cases the work is regarded as a calling or mission with Life's rewards coming from the giving.

Too often the caregiver looks for fulfillment to be handed back from other people. Happiness, Love, and fulfillment are emotions that you allow yourSelf to have when certain conditions are met. Nobody else gives you these emotions.

If you are feeling unhappy, unloved or unfulfilled you may only need to realign your thinking rather than your entire Life. Peace is only a thought away from anger.

If you've shared your Self in a positive, understandable and loving way, you have a right to feel fulfilled, regardless of how your offering was received.

If you did a good job and gave enough, release it. Mothers and caregivers need to sense when they've done enough, and stop doing. Know you've planted seeds, you've done your part and let it go from your consciousness.

The Pressures Of Emotional Intimacy

In the past the extended family, farm community, church and friends were a cohesive support system providing medical care, emotional support, food, money and child care. Today those roles are often filled by professional caregivers.

Medical people are exposed to the most personal intimacies and are the focus of both affectionate and hostile energy. The professional caregiver is often required to be surrogate mother, father or lover to many many people month after month. It is a giving role and a potentially draining one if the Caregiver doesn't take care of the Self.

Caregivers need extra tender loving care.

The Energy Drain

Most human relationships have a give and take balance, or the relationship doesn't continue. When we're not getting anything back from a friend or lover eventually we'll release the person from our Life. The therapeutic and teaching relationships go on and on with the professional resisting releasing the client because that means failure as a professional and too often as a person. Often caregivers hang on to a patient to "get his one". While the determination is admirable and sometimes pays off, if the human chemistry connection between two people isn't happening, the chances of success are slight. Often therapists fall into the transference trap, hanging onto disfunctional client/relationships because they haven't been able to hang onto personal relationships.

In most social service occupations the flow of positive emotions goes only one way - from the professional to the client. Often genuine efforts to do a "beyond the call of duty" job are met with anger and resentment.

Patients and clients often never think of saying thank you. The professional is being paid, and that's the thank you. Of course, most caregivers don't do it for the money. They could be making more money doing other things; the money is not thank you enough, and the lack of appreciation and positive feedback leave a hollow place inside. As is explained in the Solutions section, you've got to generate positive feedback.

Nurses And Burnout

The most profound and regular cases of burnout are among nurses. It isn't difficult to see why. Nurses study for years and are then treated as third-class citizens of the health world. Despite all their training nurses are the servants of physicians, lowly paid and least respected.

Nurses tend to be very idealistic about their profession and training programs present idealistic visions of nursing. Nurses truly want to help people and care deeply about their patients. Yet the reality crunch hits hard. During a one year investigation by the American National Commission for the study of Nursing and Nursing Education, 70 per cent of the staff nurses in American hospitals resigned from their jobs.

There are many factors that burn nurses out, shift working being a key one. Most nurses are women who either have a family or want one. The shifts turn the internal clock upside down so that night is day and day is a restless abyss. I've created a relaxation tape that helps shift workers adjust their internal clocks.

Nurses deserve our utmost respect. They are front line nurturers in a war against pain. Our society does not honor nurturing and nurses, while they do some of the most valuable human work I know of, they are often treated like bed pan porters. I feel ashamed at how this society treats nurses.

"I'm sorry about yesterday...sorry, really sorry."

The Reality Crunch

Nurses experience a severe reality shock when they start on a ward. Generally their expectation is crushed by reality. Virtually all nurses expect to be appreciated for their efforts only to discover that for patients, nurses are an available target for abuse and disrespect.

Gratification has to be generated by the nursing teams but too often there are personality conflicts, rivalries and tensions, responses to the negative energy absorbed from patients. Rather than supporting each other, nurses often release negative energy at each other. This can be avoided by choosing Love over fear. To learn how to *stay clear* of negative energy see pages 192-195.

One of the realities of the medical profession is that all of the patients die. When we're either getting Life right, or very wrong, we check out of these bodies. That is The Life Plan and if you become angry with it you are angry with everything. That's a lot for little old you to be angry at.

Nurses invite burnout unless they realize that people need their dis-ease in order to become better at Life.

The protection many nurses use to remove themSelf from an overwhelming situation is to detach emotions and occasionally engage in a kind of gallows humor sometimes at the expense of the patients.

In fact many nurses resent the patients, the very people they want to help. The original want and need to help is still there. The reason the person became a nurse is inside, but reality has raped many caregivers.

The hard work, shifts, resentment, hopelessness, helplessness and feelings of being trapped, shameful and guilty can infiltrate marriages, lovers and children.

Without survival tools the price of nursing can be total.

The Nursing Image

The reality crunch in nursing is profound if student nurses are not equipped. Nurses are trained to look professional, crisp, efficient and happy on the outside. These are qualities highly valued in nursing. And here is the supreme irony: nurses feel all the devastation of pain and death day after day, they feel all the turmoil of burnout, but as they look around, what do they see? Nurses looking crisp, efficient and pleasant.

What they *don't* see are nurses hurting, feeling anguished and guilty. A few nurses use the gallows humor and resentment but most maintain the *image* of a nurse.

In my experience virtually all nurses are feeling inner turmoil and trying to mask it - either with sarcasm, extreme crispness and efficiency, shows of false valor or coping mechanisms like tobacco, food or booze.

Many nurses looking valiant and crisp are secretly envying other nurses because they look so valiant and crisp.

Nurses conclude: "Most nurses seem to be doing O.K. so there must be something wrong with me. Maybe I'm too delicate; maybe I'm going crazy;maybe I'm not cut out to be a nurse."

Because most nurses are ashamed of their inner feelings they remain ignorant of the reality that they aren't alone. They blame burnout on themselves rather than knowing it is a sane response to an insane situation that powerfully affects almost everyone.

Nurses who feel inadequate and blame themselves for their feelings either quit the profession or seek professional help.

In some cases burnout results from the individuals reactions and perceptions. The person doesn't have the right survival tools for the job. In these cases a burnout workshop, reading or seeking individual therapy can be a great solution.

Burnout among nurses clearly lies in the situation. Using nurses in a terminal cancer ward as an example, we can't do much to remove the stress. All of the nurses will care for and to some degree care about people who are dying. My approach to this is purely spiritual. I like to give the nurses further insight into the death transition and how they can teach people and lead people through the door of death. One nurse who has these tools works in a veterans hospital. When the door of death is being offered, she tells their consciousness what to expect and holds their hand, giving them permission to go. These men wait to die until she is working. For her, leading people to the Light, is not draining, it is uplifting.

For nurses who want these tools I recommend the book "Life after Life" by Dr. Raymond Moody, Jr. M.D.

Solutions For Nurses

The first step is to change the focus from "What's wrong with me?" to "What can I do to make things better?"

There are many good points for nurses throughout this book, try the ones you like and let the others go. Beating Burnout for nurses primarily involves changing the mode of operating on a ward, reducing interstaff conflict and creating a more nurturing environment for nurturers.

Caring For The Nurse

Stress takes a physical toll, food fads or fanatical diets are not good. Whenever possible eat a good meal with someone else, make the meal an event. Eat slowly and stay relaxed. If a meal time is interrupted by an emergency at work be sure that meal time is reinstated later.

Most nursing programs include courses on nutrition and information on exercise yet burnt out nurses report eating fast food, fast at irregular times.

There are only a few ways to shake off the stress of a day, exercise is one of the best. The activity needs to be fun and non-competitive. A person who exercises can deal with much more than a lethargic person.

Overcoming Boredom

Nurses are seldom asked their opinion, and they may come to believe they don't have worthwhile ideas. This can't be true. Nurturing is a field that is so under developed. To teach people about the values of Self Love, nutrition, exercise, letting go of anger and fears and becoming better at Life is all within the potentials of the nurse.

The nurses who have taken my beating burnout seminars find they have so much to offer patients, more valuable than drugs or surgery. You need only read the books by Louise Hay and Dr. Bernie Siegel to realize the impact you can have on people.

There is no shortage of anger, fear or pain in our society, there is a drastic shortage of nurturing.

To Overcome Boredom

1. Investigate the possibility of working on another ward, adding variety to your job routine. Lateral job movement is a good solution for boredom.

2. Take real breaks to get away from it. Go outside, listen to a relaxation tape, read something inspiring, do some stretching, anything to nurture yourSelf. This is the purpose of a break. Ten minutes away will enable you to handle the next hours much more effectively.

3. Identify the sources of boredom or stress in your work environment. When do the feelings begin, what does it feel like? Make a list of the pressure points and create ways to eliminate the problem. Remember you are determining your reaction to everything.

4. Nursing publications can give you good knowledge and help you feel good about your nurturing work. Stay in touch with what is being written about the profession.

5. Find people to share your feelings with. Create a support group to discuss ways to make things better.

6. Sharing, discussions and some positive socializing is important in establishing a team closeness with colleagues. Infighting is a destructive coping mechanism. Forgive. People do the best with what they have to work with. Now be an inspiration, a true nurturer. That begins with nurturing, forgiving and Loving yourSelf.

8. Have a staff member or appoint yourSelf as a burnout "lookout" This person is aware of symptoms, talks easily to most people and keeps an eye on personnel.

9. Pay attention to what I've written about emotional withdrawl and dehumanization. Some nurses are so detached they are emotional zombies while others are on an emotional roller coaster. There is a happy medium and no two patients are the same. You must maintain your emotional balance.

Realize that what most patients need is Loving and nurturing from themself. You teach best by example.

For example a negative, frightened patient is allowing negative thoughts. You can ask the question "How is this behavior working for you? Is it resulting in what you really want...what you really need?" You've asked a good question and allowed the person to grow. From that point on it isn't your problem.

10. Instead of absorbing abuse while fighting to remain calm, learn to express your feelings toward patients in a positive teaching manner. If the patient is trying to make you feel bad tell them you know it and you won't accept their pain.

Expressing your inner feelings and teaching the patient that they are creating their own reality establishes a healthy relationship and results in greater well being for patients. The negative, angry patient won't get as much attention and if the patient isn't learning from their dis-ease the nurse is the person to get this lesson going. That is a very powerful role.

11. If your work is causing stress in your relationship there are counseling opportunities to develop an understanding. Even having a loved one read this chapter on nursing can result in a clearer understanding.

12. Make a list of happy times, the sweet spots in time. What elements were present in those happy times? What does happiness mean for you? How can you become a Life artist who creates beautiful moments with people and places and time? You are powerfully in control of all aspects of your reality because your reality is in your mind. Make this a more beautiful world and feel yourSelf respond. There is a very strong relationship between severity of burnout and lack of outside interests. Generate excitement for yourSelf outside of work. When there are sources of growth, joy, adventure and excitement outside of work you're expressing the parts of yourSelf that aren't expressed at work. Music, poetry, horses,

classes, art, healthy optimistic people are available to you. If you don't experience the joys of living you lose the purpose of living.

13. If you've been grouchy and negative, think of the fun of changing. Think of how you can shock people by choosing Love rather than fear. It is never too late to change, not for your patients and not for you. No one else is preventing you from changing.

14. If you are scoring high on the burnout questionnaires and don't have the energy to use the solutions, take a leave of absence. I often recommend six months. If that is shocking, think about yourSelf in six months if you don't take the leave. How bad does it have to get before you'll nurture yourSelf?

Continuing the same way deepens burnout, probably incapacitating you. Would you rather have an adventure, take another job for a while or be on the other side of hospital care?

Solutions For All Caregivers

In most training programs, the tools for helping the helper are neglected. The energy drain is a constant reality and methods for maintaining a high energy level amid fear, anger, pain or depression are ignored. Often simple rapport skills for opening clear communication are not taught.

The caregiver may interpret a simple communication problem as professional incompetence and incompetence as a human being. This is a serious mistake.

The solution may be as simple as coming out from behind a desk, learning to mirror people, or getting rid of the uniform. Many caregivers are frustrated with the lack of appreciation and feedback they get but they don't let go of the intimidation factors and alienating 'tools' of clinics.

It is hard work to play a role, to look the part, say and act the way we think a professional *should* act.

Should is a dangerous word. It is someone else's idea of what you *should* be, not your idea, not a creative idea, not a new or spontaneous idea. By letting go of the shoulds, you allow yourSelf to be a spontaneous part of all your human interactions. Your humanity enriches your work. I do not think anyone can be too human. And humanity is its own reward, its own fuel for passion.

Separating Work And Home In A Healthy Way

Having opened up humanity, you need to differentiate between working and not working. There is no set rule and each person must find a balance that works over the long run. Some people burn out because they are cold fish at work, losing the benefits of humanity. Others burn out because they're gushing emotions and intimacy all day long. You've got to find your own level of humanity.

Some patients need more humanity than others. If you are feeling unsatisfied with a professional relationship think about warming it up or cooling it off so you are more fulfilled.

Work that involves Life issues blurs the line between professional and personal. The lack of distinct separation is one of the great occupational hazards of caregivers. Too often professionals over compensate, deciding they need to be one person at work and another at home.

The separation between work and home needs to be on a personal level. Be yourSelf at work. Flow, relax, laugh and play with people. Don't separate the best parts of you, but do separate your Self worth. Your Self worth cannot be anchored to your success rate at work. Don't let the events of the day make you feel like a dirt bag at night. You'll discover some techniques for letting go of the day in the solutions section.

The Essence Of Caregiving

Ultimately people are helped or healed because they've chosen to allow themselves to be helped or they've learned to help themselves. Until the pain is bad enough they will not change and let pain go. Their choice to stay the same is their's and needn't be an energy drain on you. Allowing them their process, their pain and lessons allows you to stop punishing yourSelf for other people's choices.

Tomorrow is another day. You have the potentials of your tomorrow and they have theirs. You need not hand the rest of your today over to tomorrow. Keep today for enjoying yourSelf.

The Emotional Roller Coaster Of Caregiving

Emotional roller coaster rides are nauseating for everyone. They're particularly disruptive for we sensitive caregivers who expect to eliminate pain, and rely on healing and teaching skills to validate Life. Life is validation of Life.

We're misguided if we want to save people from pain. Yet the very people who are attracted to caregiving work are sensitive, compassionate and tender. They're people who want to be saviours. These are the people most at risk for burnout.

As caregivers, we tend to place other people's needs above our own, particularly if we think the other person is in more pain than we are.

Remember, it is their pain, it is their fear, it is their lesson. We can't save people from themselves, we can only equip them and show them what might be a better way, but ultimately you don't have anyone else's answers. How could you when you're still struggling to find your own?

Release yourSelf from the need to save people from their lessons. People need pain in order to learn and grow.

To Know And Not To Do Is Not Yet To Know

It is assumed that someone with the skills to teach or heal other people would teach and heal themself. If you can take care of other people you certainly take care of yourSelf. You do take care of yourSelf don't you?

Doctors, nurses and other caregivers are not known for taking care of themselves. What we share with other people we often forget for ourselves. Having the answers is very different from using them. Be a great Self caregiver and you'll be a great teacher. We teach best by example.

Monitor Your Peers

As is outlined in the solutions section, it is particularly important for caregivers to communicate and monitor one another. It is up to you as a colleague who knows the demands of the work, to share awarenesses of stress and burnout with people who are in trouble. Often you have to be very direct because the caregiver is used to being a provider rather than a recipient. The dynamic must be clear and the ego of the caregiver needing care must be placed aside. "Don't treat me like one of *them*", may be the response of a person who has placed themself 'above' the patients in knowledge and wisdom.

Caregivers Need Extra Care

In addition to monitoring your peers it is important to be a motivator, to encourage and instill confidence in others. By giving encouragement to others you will receive and create a more nurturing environment. Nothing burns people out faster than back-stabbing among the staff and abuse from the patients.

Dentists And Burnout

Most people are surprised to learn burnout among dentists is extremely high. On the surface dentistry seems relatively easy, lucrative and nonstressful. No one dies in the dental chair, the dentist is not part of a bureaucracy, is independent and determines the work hours. But there are several reasons most dentists experience burn out. The prime reason is that dentists are highly skilled, highly trained professionals who perform routine tasks and invariably find themselves unappreciated for their work.

Very few dentists collaborate with other dentists and the typical office staff, a receptionist, a hygienist and an assistant, don't have the expertise to discuss the merits of the work on the dentist's level. Most dentists don't collaborate, so there is no one to say "Wow what a swell job you've done capping that molar."

Certainly the patients are grateful...or are they? Most patients are primarily concerned with getting out of the dentist's office with as little pain as quickly as possible. The patients are in a high state of anxiety, many willingly admit they hate their dentist and this is communicated in many subtle and not so subtle ways. While dentists know this, they have a helper mentality, they've gone to school a long time, worked hard and incurred major debts to set up a good clinic. They didn't do it to be hated, they did it to be loved and accepted.

Very few patients ever think of the dentist's needs for respect, appreciation and approval.

Dentists work more intimately than most professionals, with the exception of gynocologists or proctologists. One of our most protected areas, the mouth is the construction zone, this not only produces physical and psychological discomfort for the patient but meaningful communication is rather limited.

Generally the patient only communicates pain or disapproval, even when the patient can see what is going on in a mirror, few people know enough to utter sounds of enthusiastic approval even when the dentist is a Barishnikov with the drill.

People almost never call their dentist after a visit to say "thanks for the great filling" or "gee, my bite is really better". If a dentist hears from a patient after a visit it is to receive a complaint.

"Promise you'll thank and respect me when it's over."

Thoughts are things and emotions are things. Anger and fear can be transferred between people and the dentist is open to both hour after hour, day after day, week after week. The dentist is very close to the patient with the chest, stomach and abdomen exposed to all kinds of panic, fear and anger. Emotions can be absorbed by all caregivers. One of our base instincts is survival. It takes a tremendous amount of negative emotions and dark, heavy energy to override the survival instincts. Suicide among dentists is extremely high. The decompression tape I've created helps caregivers release heavy emotions.

Burnout happens when effort spent is in inverse proportion to rewards received. No wonder these caregivers tend to have extreme mood swings and suffer the erosion of the spirit called job is boring, the rewards are few so they may as well get rich. They typically own large houses, expensive cars and dread going to work in the morning - waiting for the day their investments will allow them the freedom to quit dentistry.

While money is a useful commodity that buys some satisfactions, it is not a cure for burnout.

Solutions for Dentists

Dentists are bright people. They need to be informed in school that the risk of intellectual burnout is high. Many survival techniques need to be included in dental school curriculum.

It is important dentists have an understanding of body mechanics. Diseases of the bone, back problems and posture defects are common health problems. Since many dentists stand improperly for long periods of time, with their weight unevenly distributed, stress in the joints, ligaments and musculature are common complaints.

The list of physical maladies among dentists is dramatically long. Dentistry is a physically demanding job and little is being done to prepare dentists for this. Among all the professional groups in this book, dentists are the least physically fit. An understanding of the pressures placed on the dentist's body is important and can be learned through physical education departments at colleges and universities. Experts in the field are available.

Indications are that the use of a stool can prolong a dentist's career by seventeen percent. These stools are designed to relieve the problems of posture, internal constrictions and limb imbalance .

It is also important for dentists experiencing burnout to seek workshops in which positive attitudes about emotions are taught. Emotions are our barometer of Life, it is important to know how to use them. With this emotional education should be information on relaxation for the dentist and patients. When I speak to groups of dentists I cover both these subjects and include rapid hypnosis inductions. The emotional response of the patient is mirrored by the dentist. It is important for both to be calm and collected. Learning relaxation techniques in workshops or using the tapes available at the back of the book can be very helpful.

It hardly seems my place to be communicating to doctors about the values of regular exercise and good nutrition but dentists are notoriously unhealthy people. Half of the dentists who retire do so because of ill health. The most common problems are diseases of the circulatory system and the bones.

Dentists need favorite fresh fruits and juices in the office. The easiest way to keep strength up is to provide the body with food and exercise. It is important that lunch is not cut short or cut out.

Dentistry is the one profession for which I recommend having lunch with a colleague. It is great for dentists to "do lunch" without being afraid to talk shop. Light foods give you a lift at lunch so you're not in an energy lag all afternoon. After lunch is the perfect time for a short walk, to combine light exercise and relaxation.

If you decide you won't allow yourSelf to have a lunch because you'll lose income, this choice indicates you're not ready to beat burnout and it will have to get worse before you'll change.

An analysis of Life is necessary. Look at nutrition, exercise and rest, social involvements, family colleagues and intellectual stimulation. Think about your responses to the questionnaires and see how well rounded you are. Balance is necessary to beat burnout.

You can have fun and be creative in the ways you resolve the stress points in your career and your Life. Make it an adventure. Realize that positive change is fun.

Establish a dental support group and socialize with dentists to open opportunities to discuss professional challenges you're facing. You need to know what other people are doing to beat burnout.

If your relationships are troubled seek professional help quickly. Dentistry is a profession in which people choose to carry stress. What counts most is maintaining your wellness and Self esteem. If you lose either you risk losing it all.

Remember that thoughts and talk of suicide are to be taken seriously especially among dentists. Be particularly aware of any sudden happiness or changes in a person who has experienced a series of depressions. Often this signals a decision to end it all and the last few days are a relief.

Take pleasure in the little things in Life. Become a Life artist. All lives are in seasons, some seasons are of happiness and others of sorrow. Dentists are not exempt, but they are subjected to large doses of heavy emotions like fear, anxiety, and suppressed anger. Emotions are things and you can be absorbing other people's emotions. Learn to relax and clear yourSelf of heavy energies. I have a relaxation tape for dentists. It can be ordered by writing to my shipping department.

Read through the Solutions sections and be aware of the ideas that feel right and the ones that feel really wrong. Is it possible you react so negatively to a solution because it is exactly what you need?

Above all be aware of your soul and your spiritual well being. If that child within you is very unhappy, it is time to make some changes. You are worth it.

Chapter 6   Burnout Among The Scholars

Teachers

It seems like such a great job! Excellent fringe benefits, frequent vacations, most summers off, job security and the work involves young people and children.

But teachers are leaving the profession in record numbers, surveys indicate a full thirty percent would rather be doing something else.

These teachers entered the profession as sincere, dedicated and well educated people. What is happening?

Each teacher is an individual, so there aren't any pat answers, but patterns have emerged and the pressure points are clear.

The Public Challenge Of Teaching

The public perception of teaching is not a positive one. Most people consider a *summers off job* to be a lark. A teacher is often compared to a highly paid baby sitter, but for the work the money isn't all that great.   Compare the income of plumbers who install sinks and toilets to educators and see the discrepancy. Feeling under appreciated, teachers can begin to doubt their own worth and Self esteem and this is the first step on the path to burnout.

Discipline

It has been estimated that one out of every ten teachers has been physically attacked. These incidents take place on and off school property. Theft and damage of personal property is not uncommon while students pounding on each other is also on the rise. The teacher not only receives anger stemming from a miserable home, but at any time the teacher can be a fight referee.

Surveys indicate teachers are in an increasingly disruptive environment, without the ability to physically reprimand a student, parents who say they can't do anything about it and a supervisory structure that says "do the best you can" but has a reputation of looking the other way.

Combine constantly having to deal with adolescent issues, violence, school boards that cut budgets and expect superior results and students "weaned" on television and films requiring Hollywood glitz to keep their shrunken attention spans alert, and you have an understanding of the term "combat neurosis" as applied to teachers.

Lack Of Respect

There is an expression that begins with "Those who can do..." I won't finish it because it's too trite. The idea that teaching is a refuge for wimps and that anybody can teach is more evidence of a gradual but profound devaluation of education by our society.

Perhaps there is no other profession that is so criticized, held up to public scrutiny yet so nearly devoid of prestige. To be a public school teacher is to be at the bottom of the professional totem pole and it takes its toll on teacher morale.

Working Conditions

Children require supervision. While the children have recess the teacher still supervises. From the time the teacher arrives in the morning to the time they leave, they are usually in direct contact with students. Often there isn't a "safe" time to go to the toilet.

While the public perception is that teachers work short days, this ignores lunches spent supervising students, time preparing lessons and exams, marking papers, extra-curricular activities as coaches, club supervisors, and tutoring students.

There is little time to talk to colleagues without children around. There is little time for spontaneous breaks, or just a moment of privacy. The feeling of being trapped, the inability to take a walk or chat with a colleague compounds the situation.

Effective teaching requires immediate decisions, continual giving, listening, caring, patience and nurturing. In addition the teacher is being graded by everyone, supervisors, students, peers and parents.

Student Attitude

It is possible that since time began adults have regarded the youth of the day as inferior to "when I was a kid". The perception of working with a doomed generation contributes to burnout.

Children are a great mirror of a society. Disfunctions of parents, marriages and society surfaces quickly among the children. The burnout of a parent quickly spreads to a child.

Students enjoy looking like aliens. To the seasoned teacher students with shaved heads, studded leathers or heavy metal attitudes, come from a dark counter-culture.

While the students may view the teacher as hopelessly out of it, the teacher may view the students as impulsive, undisciplined, techno-crazy, disrespectful vidiots. In adversary relationships everyone suffers.

The Feeling Of Being Used

Praise is often hard to find or generate from students who are slow to appreciate authority figures. A teacher can feel used by everyone; there aren't a lot of tangible rewards. Students pass, graduate and disappear. Meanwhile there is a new gang stampeding in the door. Like all the people professions, it can feel like a factory, an assembly line. A lot of energy can go into a student but teachers rarely get to appreciate the final product.

Any bright, young, creative teacher wants to believe their contribution is important and unique. If a teacher feels like a cog in a wheel, passion fades.

Isolation

It is a puzzle why, in a profession of human relations, so little effort is put into teaching rapport skills, communications skills, learning modalities, and establishing sound human relations among colleagues, students and supervisors.

Teachers can feel very alone. It is a sad fact that many teachers don't have a trusted colleague with whom they can share the highs and lows of teaching. Instead, valuable communication time is spent discussing the politics of who is next principal, department chair, who got what equipment. Political jockeying and infighting eliminate a spirit of sharing which can nurture the soul.

The Fads Of Teaching

We love technology that promises to improve our lives. We believe that eventually everything will be solved by the invention of something. It may be a new idea or gimmick like new math, open classrooms, programmed instruction, behavioral objectives, performance contracting, workshop learning, individual instruction, mastery learning, prescription teaching, learning centres. Education can be a faddy profession.

Curriculums and educational whims are often dictated by people out of touch with classroom teaching. The constant innovations, professional developments, courses, upgrades and workshops may leave a teacher agog. People who feel confused, strained and without control burn out.

Red Tape

Systems do not change easily. Levels of governments, school boards, supervisors and principals form a complex web of regulations egos and opinion holders. The chain of command is often a twisted one, straight answers and decisions, new materials and equipment, exciting ideas, can be stalled, stopped and stomped on. It all takes its toll.

Teacher Solutions

These solutions aren't the total answer. Beating burnout requires some Self examination and the applicable solutions in the final chapters.

Constant contact with students is a serious problem. But the creative teacher has escapes. You can "buy" non-contact time.

By searching all the films, videos and resource material, including parents and people who will speak, you can generate and stockpile quiet time. Invite a graduate student back to talk to the class about their adventures with biology or math. Combine class events so another teacher can supervise during the film. A teacher who manages burnout always has a few aces in the hole for the days you don't feel like teaching. Use the resources you have and don't feel guilty.

If you're burning out it's time to brainstorm to find ways to survive. Eliminate as many pressure points as possible.

If you are overextended with extra-curricular activities find ways to lighten the load.

Don't assign more work than you can correct in one hour. Make it all efficient and easy.

If you're yelling these days get some aid, a bell, an air horn, flick the lights, anything other than having to scream. Perhaps not *anything*, a gun is not a good idea.

Leave at least two nights a week for you to do the things you enjoy and that includes nothing. These are your nights for Self indulgence and nothing gets in the way. You've got to Love yourSelf.

Exercise and food are very important. Seek a physical activity you enjoy. Make it fun and you will be amazed at how your mind and body respond. Exertion is a fantastic release. When you feel that need to go for a long walk, Go! That is your inner wisdom telling you what you need.

Grab rest time whenever you can. Listen to a relaxation tape, meditate for five minutes. Get rid of all the negative images of the day and you'll be calm and more in control.

Teach yourself not to react within a tenth of a second, as we usually do. When you see a problem say the word *relaxation* to yourSelf, wait a full two seconds and then respond. You'll find things much less tension producing.

If something is bugging you, know you've allowed it because you control your response to all things. You can let negativity work on you or you can choose peace.

After lunch is an energy lag time. The blood is in the stomach digesting. Know this, it is a fact of Life. Don't get angry with that after lunch class, do something positive, with your class take some long deep breaths and say the affirmation "I affirm I'm ready to learn".

A lethargic class can be perked up with some deep knee bends, stretching or other physical activity to get blood flowing. Be a little more up and flashy after lunch to get things moving.

Be Interesting

Teachers who lead interesting lives make interesting teachers, so do interesting things, have adventures! Stop moaning and realize you are creating your Life. Become an expert in something, get passionate about Life. Stay a student of Life.

If there is a problem in your school then find a resource person, a book, an answer. Set up an in-service workshop for your school. Invite someone who has answers.

Seek out trusted people to talk to. Often teachers are moved from school to school. If there isn't anyone in your present school, you probably haven't looked very hard, but you can call that teacher friend from the previous school. Get together for a talk but don't let it become a bitch session.

Be an active agent in your school and your Life rather than feeling like a pawn being shoved around and used.

Brighten Up Your Life

Most classrooms are dull places, why not make your environment stimulating? Bring photos of your heroes and put them on the walls. Get photos of students you've influenced and post them where you can see your impact. Fill your work spaces with beauty, flowers, posters, stimulation.

Streamline the way you grade and mark students. Make it fast and efficient and as often as possible go home without school-related tasks. If this is a scary idea then you'd better think about filling up your home and night Life with fun.

Use the decompression tape I've made, or find decompression activities.

Effective people say no. You can't help everyone and be everywhere so allow people their Life lessons. You've learned students have to struggle to achieve, so do adults.

It is great for teachers to take an occasional trip where nobody knows you and expects you to act like a teacher. Then have fun.

Getting What You Want

To discover what you really want and can do to get it take a piece of paper and set up three columns. Head them this way.

I feel stress from:	*I can get what I want by:*	*I can avoid the stress by:*

Fill in the columns by brainstorming. Let your mind go and write down even the silly ideas. Silliness can result in something brilliant. Follow this guide you've created and see how well it works for you.

People burn out because they lose sight of their own ability to change. You don't have to do the same stuff over and over again. Don't do things the same, introduce some theatre to your teaching, find ways to play with the subject you're teaching. If it is fun for you it will be fun for them.

You can learn a lot about happiness by making a list of the happiest, most wonderful experiences you've ever had. These are the sweet spots in time. They don't happen by accident, they are created by people. Become a Life artist, create sweet spots with people and places and time.

It is vitally important to read through all the solutions sections and form a plan for yourSelf. Highlight or makes notes beside the suggestions that will work for you. Try new things and post notes to remind yourSelf you're changing. Why not post a note saying "I'm changing" or "What can you do to love you today?" across from a place you might sit every morning. And take loving care of your Soul, you're worth it.

Student Burnout

The student days... often considered to be "the best years of our lives". A time to experiment, try new ideas and experiences, a time of intellectual and physical stimulation. It is a time of discovering, learning and social development.

But all is not so rosy. Suicide is the second leading cause of death among the college-age young. Accidents are the number one cause of student death, and many may not be so accidental.

It seems that "the best years" are often spent dealing with stress, competition, alienation and failure.

Problems In The Study Hall

The pressures of college life are real. While some students are on an educational lark, others in intense programs are pitted against every person in their class. Every classmate is a threat. Trust is harshly tested and most students cut themselves off in subtle little ways.

External pressures from classes, deadlines and assignments are not the problem, internal pressures smother souls.

Consider the pressures of entering a program and finding the base requirements more demanding than imagined. Long term goals are riding on this and students aren't in this just for themselves, they are in it for parents, friends, neighbors, grandparents, past teachers and for the good of all.

The student's existence is rocked by each exam, each paper. Only the best will enter the graduate programs and fulfill professional dreams. One bad mark may make it unattainable.

Everything rides it.

Even for those who succeed, the pressures, and the costs of being at the top exact a price.

Change And Isolation

Old friends, those who didn't make the grade are out of the running. New friends must be found. The social glue for friendship has changed, social patterns have changed.

The responsibilities for achieving, for eating and surviving, for getting things done well and on time, for managing money are for the first time on the shoulders of the student. Often the parents are vocal about how much this education is costing. The student is supposed to be independent, but in the face of emotional reminders they are dependent. A young, sensitive person can feel adrift.

Students have very little power. They are subordinates to the wishes whims, personalities and dictates of their professors. They are forced to study topics and outdated documents that have no value in tomorrow's world. Colleges and universities are a business. Much of what is learned is of no real value but it keeps the head counts up.

To succeed students must be sensitive and aware. Their mind is in a record mode. It doesn't matter whether the information feels right, it must be remembered and regurgitated as given. Students are rewarded, not for interpreting or creating, they are rewarded for having an efficient mental filing system. Students are not supposed to think they are supposed to remember.

Something creative, new, innovate and challenging isn't accepted as worthwhile in schools because the purpose is to know what has been done, not what can be done.

Creative, innovative or wise people do not make good students. Passive, obedient, rememberers make good students.

The student deals with many professors and tutorial leaders, each with a different understanding of teaching, learning and the subject at hand. The student must adapt to the professor, not the other way around. There is very little cohesiveness in higher education.

The demands are real. The student leaves home, family and friends, enters a socialized system, struggles with financial concerns - guilt over too much money, fear over too little. The student is seeking a personal and sexual identity, all in the face of mastering abilities, skills and knowledge while being told they are not mature enough to doubt, challenge or reject what is being taught. And I've hardly touched on making it as a desirable love object on Saturday nights.

Is it any wonder the primary killers of students are accidents and suicide?

Students push themselves to meet the many demands of college life but the most damaging demands are Self imposed needs to achieve scholastically, to party and have fun because these are supposed to be "the best years" and the need to keep an awareness of Self and values intact. The question "Who am I" can reveal a void while struggling to stay a cork in the river of higher education.

An inability to concentrate is an early burnout signal. Staring off into space is common. Random thoughts creep in all the time and everything becomes very general, very generic.

Many burning out students find themselves bored, feeling useless, critical and cynical. They become emotionally self pitying, throwing lavish pity parties and wallowing in the negativity of everything. They often rule out the possibility that anyone else can help. They've lost faith in their own abilities and the abilities of others so they cut themselves off even more, blaming others for their troubles.

An extra assignment can send them on a crying jag. Burning out students tend to have outbursts of anger, they are irritable, desperate and often paranoid.

LSD, crack, cocaine, marijuana, alcohol are all easy to obtain and well advocated among students. Drugs cloud the mind and affect the student's ability to think clearly, reason things out and solve problems. The stresses and paranoia compound to create more emotional strain experienced through an exhausted mind. This is when the chance of serious substance abuse is greatest.

Things outside the college seem to be of more worth than what they are experiencing. The past becomes safer than the present and some simply go through the motions. They don't value their experience. They are memorizers.

Some drop out, in search of a way to be useful in the world. They become enemies of education.

For the student who can't see that there are opportunities, ways to change, ways to make things easier, suicide is the tragic choice. College and Life seem useless and too tragic to continue. Suicide is the ultimate pity party.

It is important for students who see friends in a prolonged pity party to send them to a counselor or at least give them this book.

Beating Student Burnout

We are not humans having a spiritual experience, we are spirits having a human experience. We need to keep the insanities of education and society in perspective. Both are artificial and temporary realities. If we forget about Life, Nature, our true refuge, Schoolhouse Earth and the *Big Picture* by taking total refuge in a manmade reality, we're selling our soul. Diplomas, degrees and job titles are only labels indicating achievement among the normal. It's never worth killing yourSelf over.

True success...Cosmic significance, isn't a group enterprise and it is freely available to all who seek IT.

Mothers Are Smart

We need to eat good food, exercise and get enough sleep. These things significantly reduce burnout. There are no better places for a variety of healthy foods and athletic facilities than college campuses. The endorphin released by exercise is the ultimate feel good drug.

Anyone who parties hearty and lasts for the duration rests before and after partying, it helps you keep a perspective.

To avoid intellectual burnout it is best to do readings and essays as they come up. Don't put it off until panic time. Panic is avoided by pacing yourSelf.

Always have an exciting course on the go. Select the best professors and involve yourself in learning groups. The energy and optimism of enthusiastic people will carry you along.

There is help. Problems with drugs, sex, health or relationships are why counselors are on campus. There is help and you owe it to that child within you, to find it.

Values are very important to you. You've been bombarded with values since you were born. Your parents, schools, friends, the media, movies all these things influence you. So what do you value?

The values exercise can help you find out what is really important to you. It is critical to be putting your energy into things that you value. Don't feel guilty about it. Enjoy what you value. Values evolve, parents have evolved into their set of values and students have another set of values. Our values don't stay the same, so if you value fun don't feel guilty.

It is great to post notes to yourSelf. Put your top values up in your room to remind you of what you need and value.

If school is too much then don't drop out, stop out! Leave for a time, travel, have an adventure, get a job, "do your thing".

Students who stop out have a much better time when they return. Many colleges are recommending people stop out for a semester.

Life Is IT

Society and education have complicated living. As a hypnotherapist who interviews souls, I've learned that suicide is never a solution. I absolutely know that this is Schoolhouse Earth, where souls come to learn the lessons of Loving, Sharing, Forgiveness, Faith and Humility.

Everything is about Life and when anyone terminates their Life they'll have to go through it again, and the next time there may not be so much freedom. I know we keep coming back until we get Life right. You can learn the lessons of Life now, or you can put them off for the next time.

Doesn't it make sense to become good at Life now?

Chapter 7   Lawyers & Burnout

Lawyers are like everyone else, they want to be loved and accepted. But the profession is one of dilemmas.

Some lawyers are highly respected, rewarded and well placed in business and politics but the general attitude toward lawyers isn't very positive. Lawyer jokes almost always involve cheating someone out of money. Lawyers are widely viewed as crooks in three piece suits and this strong negative public bias takes a toll.

Law schools are populated by energetic, bright people with a dream. They have ideas about helping people and having positive impact on lives and society. But the bubble bursts quickly.

Lawyers are often abused and not trusted by the people they represent. The young lawyers' expectations of professional and public respect is not fulfilled. It turns out to be a profession not at all as they imagined.

Every time a lawyer is caught breaking the law it is widely publicized. To the public it is like an athlete missing the play on purpose. When a lawyer bends and breaks the law the public feels violated.

Most of the work for young lawyers is repetitive, dull and minor. Those socially conscious souls who join legal service organizations can find themselves unable to make significant improvement in their client's lives. Even when they win a case nothing much changes for the client and another case is waiting to eradicate the victory.

Many clients are motivated by revenge or greed. They don't clearly know what they expect the lawyer to do yet the lawyer has to build a worthwhile case, often in a situation where the fee is more worthwhile than the case.

Conflict is not uncommon between client and lawyer and because the lawyer is logical rather than passionate or enraged the client interprets professionalism as disinterest.

The Values Conflicts

Lawyers tend to be decent, law-abiding people with friends and families. They don't enjoy hurting or humiliating people but they do value total victory. They have been taught to prove a point beyond a doubt whether it means humiliating, emotionally devastating, degrading or psychologically shattering an innocent witness.

Harsh treatment of witnesses conflicts with human values and damages Self worth and Self image, no matter how experienced the lawyer is, it takes a toll.

The dilemma of defending a guilty party bleaches the lawyer's personal sense of fairness and justice. A good lawyer has to strive to prove the innocence of guilty people, to pull out all the stops knowing the client was in the wrong and has the potential to harm other people again. The lawyer may know of deviant, criminal behavior, be successful in winning the case and know that someone will probably be raped or killed because this person is free.

The conflicts of values can be devastating.

Lawyers also have conflicts over fees. They take the money often wondering if what they've done merits the amount. If a case violates a personal sense of fairness or justice, the problem is compounded and Self respect is further damaged.

The Personal Conflicts

The average work year for associate lawyers is 2,100 hours, or forty-two hours a week for fifty weeks. Lawyers in legal services handle from 250 to 500 more cases per year than those in private practice.

Too much time is spent away from Life. Relationships, families, even a simple dinner, can become a source of friction. And when the lawyer arrives home irritable, tired and tending to think about work, it eats away at Love.

Without a satisfying personal Life there is little balance or recharging energy.

The Critical Edge

Public criticism of lawyers can be traced back as far as Plato, who wrote of their "unrighteous souls." Media coverage and articles citing lawyers as ambulance chasers and whiplash specialists are not rare. The roles of lawyers in public scandals like Watergate don't help to endear the profession to anyone.

The result is that lawyers can doubt their own sincerity and honesty.

Bearing Bad News

Attorneys often have to share bad or devastating information clients may not want to know. Uncovering personal information upsets families and careers. Plus the profession has created an elitist attitude, a difficult writing and communications style, and jargon and court proceedings that, to the lay person, look more like jockeying and maneuvering than truth and justice.

Many believe the successful lawyer is the "trickiest" most accomplished liar. In addition many published studies, including public statements by Chief Justice Warren Burger in

1977, indicate many lawyers are not qualified to do an adequate job.

In spite of studies which show most lawyers are well qualified, the damaging statements stay branded into everyone's memory.

The Problem Of Training

Many lawyers feel their training inadequate. They feel poorly equipped in communication, rapport and practical skills that they need on a daily basis.

Like anyone in the people helping professions, clients are angry, upset, emotional, depressed, confused and scared. If rapport and trust are not established with clients and witnesses, bonding doesn't happen. Emotional intensity during a trial is exceptionally high and constant exposure to fundamental human problems like unemployment, alcoholism, poverty, and other things that lawyers don't fix has a frustrating and draining effect. It leads to dehumanization, treating clients like things, or it can lead to emotional exhaustion. Few law schools teach emotional survival techniques and the reality crunch hits hard and doesn't let up.

Lawyers also complain of spending too much time in school on landmark cases, and not enough time on how to efficiently prepare a case for trial. Young lawyers spend inordinate amounts of time preparing cases and resenting the job while sacrificing personal lives and heading for burnout.

Poor Management

Most law firms are poorly managed. Expectations of young associates are often unclear. Different partners have different expectations and lawyers are not great communicators. The egos, roles and jargon get in the way.

To work on some interesting cases the young associate has to perform and compete, but feedback and approval don't flow easily. The results of having to be competitive yet not knowing how you are doing can be overwhelming. The feeling of being used and abused creeps in and morale plummets.

Overworked with too many clients and too many boring cases and without clear professional growth opportunities, many associates begin to spin their wheels, falling behind trying to get ahead. Opportunities for courses and enriching experiences are often not provided because of time limits and the attorney begins to feel stagnant. Without growth and real opportunities self-image suffers, passion sputters, the goals blur and confidence drops.

Law partners are not great managers or motivators. They tend not to be great employers.

Solutions For Lawyers

Initial solutions are the obvious ones. Take care of your body. Exercise, eat well and rest. Make your exercise and meal times as important as your clients. Without one you aren't much good for the other. Make time for eating and loving other people. These are necessary elements of living. Meals should be social events.

Limit coffee intake, it is a stressor. Keep small cans of juice, fruit, seeds or nuts on hand at the office. Switch to decaf or at least half decaf coffee. According to stress expert Dr. Peter Hanson, as little as two and a half cups of coffee per day will double the adrenalin in your bloodstream, at a time when your body is already delivering adrenalin during stress. In addition, coffee aggravates stomach ulcers and when you are under stress the stomach shuts down, giving acidic coffee even more time to damage your stomach lining. Coffee also contributes to hemorrhoids, heart disease, colitis and angina.

Avoid alcohol at lunch, it saps energy and reduces your ability to deal with stress. A light lunch will keep you aware and productive in the afternoon.

Lawyers spend a lot of time sitting, exercise is not to be forgotten and the endorphin released during physical activity is the best drug you'll find.

Relaxation techniques and tapes are a great help in reducing the mental effects of being a lawyer. The tapes I've made can be ordered from the back of this book.

Seeking A Balanced View Of The Profession

To counteract lack of respect, read positive articles on the profession. These positive approaches to law demonstrate that you are in a profession that deserves and in many cases has more respect than is generally believed. Seek out articles that give a balanced view of the profession.

There are many seminars for developing interpersonal and communication skills. In my burnout workshops I always pass on the tools that have helped me in my clinic. Rapport skills can be developed by anyone at any age. Many colleges and open universities offer communication and rapport courses. It is never too late to learn.

It is smart to be aware of the ruts, to not always do the same tasks at the same time. Organize a day for variety, open yourself to experiencing different aspects of law.

Rather than letting the telephone or whims of others control you, take control of your day . You might designate no calls hours. People will quickly learn when they won't be able to reach you.

Lawyers and their egos make them the most unlikely candidates to go through the questionnaires in this book. Self awareness can help a great deal. If you know the stress points, hassle factors and causes of your personal burnout you are in a position to know what solutions work for you.

Know What Is Expected Of You

Chances are you are your own worst taskmaster, putting more pressures and expectations on yourSelf than anyone else. Inquire of your partners or supervisors exactly what is expected of you. They assumed the role of manager/employer and it's important they deal with the people who work for them. Make a list of the skills needed to meet their expectations and develop the skills that are missing. There are excellent courses and seminars, books, associations and peer groups. If you are committed to beating burnout you won't let your schedule prevent professional or personal growth.

Emotional Time Out

When stress is heaviest, efficiency drops. Situations are not filled with stress, people are. Stress isn't out there, it is something you allow inside. If you feel stress, think the words *I choose peace* repeat the words several times internally.

Often people are dumping their crisis, sense of failure or inadequacy into your lap. You can hold onto their emotional crap or affirm that you won't absorb it and let the crap drop on the floor. The choice is yours. If you absorb the negative energy or emotions of others, see the sections on anger.

It is important to have a decompression or unwind state. This can be in your office lying on the floor, with a secretary/guard posted outside, it can be in a bathroom, in a parking lot or in a park. Establish a state of unwind for yourSelf and use this when the going gets tough. Don't just plough through tough times adding this stress to your internal library of emotional horrors. Get rid of it as it happens. People who accumulate tension, stress and anger tend to lose it in hospitals. Carrying anger, fear or guilt results in dis-ease. Taking on the emotions of a peer or a client doesn't help anyone.

If you have trouble unwinding see the section on decompression.

Be Human

It is always best to be honest and open with clients. Letting them know you have a heavy case load is good. It opens you as a human being and generates trust, breaking down barriers and humanizing the relationship. It is not necessary to project an aura of total competence and emotional detachment. This sanitized role is damaging to relationships with clients and to your abilities to function over the long term. If your lawyer act is fake then stop acting. I'm not suggesting dumping your problems on clients, I'm saying human is all you are ever going to be, so be honest with everyone and you'll be more honest with yourSelf.

Look For Burnout

Be aware of burnout symptoms in colleagues, secretaries and junior attorneys. Since most clients aren't emotionally supportive, remember that people in your office need to support each other. You might set up a colleague club or meetings in which people can talk about their challenges. Problems will be eliminated before they're debilitating.

Many lawyers have large egos, they don't share with each other and have an "it couldn't happen to me" attitude. Would you carry this book through your office allowing other people to see you're reading a book on burnout? If your answer is no then you're among the people who closet their traumas. Come on in, join humanity, it is a lot warmer.

Through the values exercise you can realize the value of your personal relationships or marriage. If it has high value it deserves to be a priority, and you deserve what it can give you in they way of intimacy, honesty and caring. Ultimately the best things in Life aren't on the job, they are Life's little rewards. It is what we do with each other as souls that matters.

Your spouse might consider forming a *spouses of lawyers* group to gain understanding of the pressures of the work and ways to be a better spouse.

Boost YourSelf

It is important to keep reminders of the successes in your Life. If you've got letters from satisfied or grateful clients, pictures of people you've helped, awards or acknowledgements keep them out and look at them on the dark days. You need reminders of the sweet spots in time.

If you don't remember many "sweet spots in time", make a list of the reasons to stay in the profession. Is there enough fulfillment? Can you generate more fulfillment by making some changes? What needs to be changed in order for you to be happy? If you don't have answers maybe a career change should be considered.

Togetherness in your office, becoming an inspiration, being human and enjoying the victories are all important ways to beat burnout. Being part of a team gives a sense of meaning, belonging and celebration to the experience of being a lawyer. Your peers will be more interested in you when you're more interested in them. Anyone can be an inspiration to other people simply by choosing to be.

I suggest you read the solutions chapters and the sections on management and bureaucrats for more insights into beating burnout.

Chapter 8   Women And Burnout

Balancing the careers of a homemaker and a professional is like moving two bicycles at the same time. You have to ride one or the other and if the road gets bumpy you've got to let the other bicycle fall.

For women trying to derive fulfillment from both their domestic role and their career the conflict is a major cause of burnout. Many women feel they've failed at both.

Homemakers' Work Stress

Homemaking is the largest single occupation on the planet. Although homemaking isn't very honored and the goods and services aren't accounted for in the gross national product, it is a vital part of our economy to say nothing of the Life process.

Housewives are, for the most part, adrift and besieged. Traditionalists on one hand say the greatest pleasures come from nurturing and caring for the needs of others, that there is honor in making a home for a husband, and family. On the other side are the messages that say satisfying personal potentials and needs are vital too.

Surveys indicate that almost twice as many housewives as employed wives say they are dissatisfied with their lives. More housewives claim they've not had a fair opportunity in Life and want their daughters to be "mostly different from themselves."

A housewife's workday doesn't end. There are rarely tangible rewards or social connections. Housework is largely undefined, it requires effort, affords little recognition and is sometimes described by husbands as "doing nothing all day".

But the wife is expected to continue staying home *"doing nothing"* while the domestic affairs magically take care of themselves.

As a result, fulfillment and rewards are vague. Housewives have an uncertain idea of their role or how good they are at it and since nobody else seems to honor it they don't either.

In the past housewives were part of a more defined group. They shared a social network with mothers, relatives and friends. Within this group there was discussion, emotional support and little doubt whether someone was a good homemaker. In the 90s mobility and working women have made housewife networks more difficult to maintain.

Women often become isolated, staying at home going crazy looking at the walls, floors and escapist television shows.

The popular media often portray the housewife as neurotic, bored, depressed or anxious with the results of being a housewife becoming "sick".

It's been described as like "being in a jail", but most studies indicate less unhappiness in the home. The women who don't want to work outside the home are generally happy, healthy and comfortable in their role. They fill their days with tasks about the house, as well as hobbies and friends. They have husbands with a comfortable income, enjoy time for themselves, and they feel in control of their lives. But since this is a book about burnout I assume it is being read by less than happy housewives.

Why Housewives Burn Out

Women exhibiting "neurotic housewife syndrome" are at high risk of burnout. They're chronically exhausted and emotionally drained. Their days spent with children make their world and their minds "shrink". Life seems empty and meaningless and the anger surfaces as depression.

Often coping mechanisms like an eating disorder, smoking, alcoholism or child abuse will develop. The addicted housewife is sending out a cry for help.

Housewives who aren't burning out measure low on the stress and burnout scales, they take pride in their role as wife and mother. They are creative about their homemaking tasks, take adult education classes and are involved in social or political issues. They feel their lives are full and have meaning.

In the burnout cases the woman tends to have to keep within a tight budget without much room for Self nurturing. She envisioned her life differently, with ideas of personal fulfillment and potentials that aren't being realized. Burnouts feel demeaned by their domestic role and they're restless and angry at their perceived lack of freedom .

Making The Most of Homemaking

It is possible to beat the burnout trend but it requires a change of attitudes and some effort. It doesn't require a lot of money. Women required to be full time homemakers for a number of years can make the most of the time by taking interest in domestic tasks and doing them efficiently. Efficiency results in free time you've created for yourSelf. With that time why not take adult education classes, do community work, attend seminars, continue an artistic or musical passion or indulge yourSelf in something you've thought would be interesting. There are others who will take care of your children while you are taking care of yourSelf if you return the favour.

Taking a day off is very important. When you can, have lunch with a friend, tour the city, walk in nature, and most important, arrange a support system of other homemakers like yourself. Find a purpose for the group and have some fun together. You can talk about your stresses but look for resolutions to the problems, don't let it become a pity party.

Wallowing in negativity only makes you feel more negative. Positive, caring support can prevent a descent into serious depression.

If you're using tranquilizers, alcohol or food to cope, get some help. Call your local YWCA, hospital or Alcoholics Anonymous to locate the organization that deals with your problem.

If you value your marriage, your home or your children get some help now. Why wait until you're flat on your face, or more desperate before you decide to get better. It is very hard on your children to witness your descent and remember you're teaching them Self destructive behaviors.

Working Women's Stress

The stereotype feminine attributes of being caring, aware, sensitive, instinctive and nurturing, result in a disproportionate number of women in the helping occupations. Women are the majority in the teaching, nursing, counselling, social work and social welfare professions, professions that involve intense, painful and emotionally demanding situations.

Many of these women are also homemakers, expected to be empathetic, understanding and sensitive to the needs of others at work and at home, around the clock. Being in a helping profession and having a family is a double drain on personal resources.

The women who are drawn to the helping professions tend to be particularly affectionate, caring, empathetic and sensitive to the needs of others. In addition client-centered professions set up the role of professional as mother, client as child. This "mothering" role is natural, nurturing and very important in our society, but there is always more a "good" mother could do and this *never enough* dynamic is a source of guilt for many women.

You Are Not A Human Doing, You Are A Human BEing

When what we've done is never enough we never stop *doing*, our batteries run down and we burn out. Being is very different from always doing. BEing is relaxed, peaceful, calm, trusting and much better than doing.

If a woman is a professional motherer the realities of work can be very frustrating. Work isn't always fair, the suffering and passivity can be very painful if Self worth is linked to mothering abilities. We must know when enough is enough and release people to their lessons. As a person burns out it is normal to feel numb to other's needs, to resent people. The impact of this on a motherer can be devastating. She feels herself resenting and even hating people for what they've done to her. Of course we allow things to be done to us. By Mothering the world, too many women turn themselves into vulnerable emotional punching bags that people in pain feel invited to punch at.

The burnt out caregiver usually resents everyone in her professional and personal Life because they "allowed this" or "made this happen" to her. It is often a long hard road for her to realize she burned herSelf out. Other people assumed she would use her common sense, nurturing and Loving skills on herSelf. When she didn't and burned out, everyone was surprised.

It can take a long time to trust people again, when in fact the burned out caregiver needs to reestablish trust in herSelf and to develop the ability to say no. She is being offered an opportunity to develop the wisdom to allow other people their pain, their process and to allow them to stumble and fall just as she allowed herself to fall. Everything is a lesson.

Women Who Don't Burn Out

The type of woman who is able to work without burning out has, Self awareness. The more Self aware and Self nurturing a woman is, the more she creates opportunities for Self expression. Women who are in touch with their wants and values are better equipped to deal with professional pushes and pulls and don't burn out as often. The more Self expression they experienced the less burned out they were. This Self expression can come from people skills, rapport skills, keeping the mind active, learning, loving, creating and celebrating Life. She is in touch with herSelf, her instincts, her human needs and knows how to Live and say no without guilt. She is not competitive, back stabbing or hateful.

Women who look for rewards and fulfillment from the "system" are often cynical and burnt out. The message is to find your own fulfillment and not expect it to come from the "higher ups" in the work place.

Men see their career as a series of steps leading upward to recognition and rewards, whereas women are less concerned with advancement.

Being low on the totem pole in terms of financial rewards and prestige is a high burnout factor among men but not for most women.

One of the great burnout factors among women is the protector aspect of mothering. We can't protect people from themselves. We can't protect people from Life. Men tend to take a "let them find out for themselves" attitude while women want to protect everyone from harm.

Ultimately people learn lessons by doing. Mother birds push the baby birds out of the nest so they will learn to fly.

A child has to feel something hot in order to know what being burned feels like. We can't protect anyone from Life and when we do they resent us for it.

This strikes at the essence of mothering, but you know how uneasy you become when a mother stifles you, over-protects you and destroys the joys of Life's adventures. Life is IT! Allow everyone to have their joys and sorrows.

"Yes...she is very much her own man."

The Double Bind Of The Professional Woman

College students participating in a study conducted by Ayala Pines looked at a videotaped interview with a woman who discussed her history, education, background and interests. One version ended with her discussing her career plans which included a university teaching position, and publishing scientific articles. The second version ended with her discussing only her family plans, saying she wanted to stay home with her child, work in the house and the garden.

The college students were shown only one version and asked for their impressions of the woman. All the students saw the same introduction which established her abilities but those who saw the career oriented tape used words like aggressive, dominant and independent; adjectives traditionally associated with males or "ball breaking" females.

By contrast students who saw only the family tape described her as dependent, less active, less ambitious, passive and less able to withstand pressure. A woman's choice to have a family seems to automatically drop her competence levels.

Women who saw the tapes gave the career woman more compliments than the house woman but men liked the family woman, citing her as more feminine, open-minded, sincere, intelligent, kind, well adjusted, sensitive, warm and determined. Men also wanted to spend more time with the family woman.

The woman who stays home is, for men, more understandable, more "normal" and less threatening.

The professional woman is still in a doomed if she does and doomed if she doesn't society. If she chooses a career she will be seen, especially by men, as less feminine, less likable and less desirable. If she chooses a family she will be seen as less vibrant, less intelligent and less competent.

In the 1990s we're seeing more women who choose not to have the family. They've avoided the dual role conflict. In other cases the home role is shared 50/50 between male and female but this tends to slide to the woman carrying more of the domestic load, resulting in conflict at home and work.

The Single Parent

The essence of beating burnout for the single parent lies within releasing the ideals. You do not have to be superprofessional, supermom or dad or superhomemaker. Life doesn't come in "ideals", it comes in days and there are horrific days for everyone. You've got to keep yourSelf together and the best way is to decide when enough mothering is enough, allow other people to fend for themselves, relax and do something for yourSelf.

Having to excel in three potentially full-time roles results in frantic activity and a sense of failure throughout.

Because of the high divorce rate, I think it is wise for everyone to ask themself before having a child, *Am I really prepared to support this child on my own*. Marriage isn't the guarantee it was in the agricultural era and we're approaching a time when nearly half the children in America come from single parent homes.

These are the days of the time famine and nobody feels it more than single parents. Everything is speeded up. In 1922 Emily Post suggested that the proper mourning time for a mature widow was three years. Fifty years later, Amy Vanderbilt urged that the bereaved be about their normal business within a week or so.

America is running out of time and oddly, the social institution that has collapsed because of it is the family. The increasing rarity of the full-time homemaker has done more to eat away at everyone's leisure time than any other factor.

The single parent can spend a lot of time buying time, and unfortunately the American dream - which is all about appearances and possessions - is something single parents do not release easily.

The full time employee/part time parent is at high risk of burnout if the true values of childhood and Life are not prioritized.

Making an appointment is one way to relate to a child but the very culture of children, playing, freedom, spontaneity, hanging-around, can collapse under the weight of a single parent's hectic schedule. Kids know when they are being cheated out of childhood. The parent is their prime role model and if being an adult means being harassed, overworked, scattered, frustrated, sick, tired and resentful of the way Life has turned out, the child isn't going to want to be an adult or be with that adult. If a parent is miserable about Life, the child will rebell against that parent. Ask yourSelf, what does a miserable person have to teach you?

We must remember the importance of play, that the sweet spots in time are not about money, they are about people and Loving.

We're now seeing depression in children accompanied by a sense that adults don't care about them. This was inconceivable 35 years ago.

Of course the single parent cares a lot, but to the child it appears distorted. The eager parent arrives home late to pour a day's attention into a child who is more ready to be tucked in than talked at.

The loss of playing and leisure time in adults filters down to the child as pressure to do things quickly for peak achievement.

If parents see their role as an investment of their precious time and money, the children may be treated as products to be improved and completed rather than special individuals to be nurtured at their own pace.

Children naturally become victims of merchandised happiness, fashion and *stuff* and the unaware single parent, who could be teaching there isn't happiness in the stuff, may be working even harder to pay for it all. What a child needs most is time, your time.

Which is most important? Having all the things people are supposed to need to be happy? A bigger home? A college education for the child? A life in the big city? Time for living and loving? Perhaps you can do the values exercise for Life and have your child do it too, then compare values.

Also try the values exercise for Home. One single parent who has coordinated my seminars in Toronto discovered that for her, home means a quiet, safe place... for her daughter home means a place for experimentation and weirdness... for her son it is a place where things can be very relaxed, scattered and comfortable... in other words messy.

This single mother had been feeling she was living with aliens but the values exercise helped everyone realize and honor each others values of home.

I wish I had a magic formula for single parents, I don't, but it is vital for the child to know the parent as something besides their provider.

When you die what do you want your children to say at your funeral? A single parent I asked this question to answered "I don't want them to say I was a good worker or provider".

Some suggestions for single parents are to watch less TV, shop by phone, buy low maintenance clothes and appliances, live in a low maintenance home and take a more lax attitude toward housekeeping.

No two days are the same, each day comes to us an original, so expect there to be moments of surprise, seeming disorder and apparent imbalance.

Burnout can be a saviour for the single parent, it affords an awareness that societies values are crazy and take a heavy toll on the soul. Single parents often talk about sleep the way a hungry person talks about food. But with too little sleep there are too few dreams. For adults and children Life must include some slow ice-creamy afternoons of laughs and cuddles and play, of favorite stories and grassy feet. Some things are just worth the time.

My motto is, when the going gets tough... relax and make loving choices.

No Is A Loving Answer

It is important to be assertive, to learn to say no when people need to learn or do something for themSelf. Without time for yourSelf you're not any good for anyone, the balance must be achieved. In a recent Burnout seminar a real estate sales person told the group she is burning out because she can't say no. People keep taking advantage of her. I told her she can say no by simply saying I have other plans or another appointment. I suggested she make appointments with her Self and keep them. But I could see from her body language that she wasn't accepting these tools for saying no, so I asked her what would have to happen for her to learn to say no. She looked at me and said "I'll probably have to die".

It is tragic that so many people choose death rather than change.

Problem Children

When you have children who do not Love themselves, or Life, it is a good time to look at yourSelf. They are a computer absorbing everything they experience and you are their major programmer. If you don't Love, care for and nurture yourSelf how can that child know to Love and approve of themSelf. If you eat junk food, smoke, criticize, moan about Life and think thoughts of scarcity you are teaching your child burnout and misery.

Your thoughts expand and create your reality. Your thoughts become your child's thoughts. If you hate your job your Life and yourSelf is it any wonder you might see pain in your child? If you criticize the child's other parent you are criticizing the child.

We tend to give our children everything we didn't have as a child, but we forget to give them the things we did have. Money is no reason to be miserable; playing, loving, celebrating and enjoying Nature are the sweet spots in time, and having them doesn't need to cost much, but missing them will make a millionaire poor.

There are great benefits in knowing what you really value. Do the values exercise for the major areas of your Life and you may find the things you really value aren't for sale. Know where you get your fulfillment and place your energies there.

At the first sign of a day going out of control realize you are out of control. You've never controlled a day in your Life but you have controlled your response to the day. Take yourSelf aside and ask your inner wisdom for guidance. Listen and follow your wisdom to what is of the highest good.

Chapter 9: Preventing Burnout

The key to beating burnout is disarming the bombs before the fuses are lit. This means getting a head start, but it is popular to believe, "If it ain't broke, don't fix it." So we wait until things 'get broke' and then we'll set to fixing them.

Unfortunately, people break down slowly, the process is personally painful and spouses, children, clients and organizations suffer. Good, talented achievers, become alcoholics, drug addicts or abusers. Too often we don't notice that people are 'broke' until they're in trouble with the law.

The bottom line in most professions is rarely the well being of the people who do the work. We tend to have much better maintenance programs for our machinery than we do for ourselves.

As a consultant to hospitals, social organizations, police forces, education systems and sales teams, I can offer the type of information I've shared in this book but the energy required to care for and rehabilitate the burnt out is three times what it requires to prevent burnout.

According to Dr. Peter Hanson, author of "Stress For Success" companies should be concentrating on extending their stress reduction programs to all those who need it. "The payback in reducing sick and absentee time and increasing productivity is incredible. For every dollar invested in preventative medicine, the return can be as much as five dollars."

Social organizations like hospitals and police forces are good at dressing people to look the part, training them to perform the role and equipping them with the tools of the job. The stage is set, but Self preservation is rarely a part of the training.

Forewarned Is Forearmed

"Why didn't anybody tell me it would be like this?" the most common words of the burnt out. People were given the uniform, the training and the tools but not the truth. They weren't told about the emotional stress of their job or how to get through it day after day after day without profound personal damage.

A lawyer who burned out after four years of working says, "I was trained in law, but not how to survive working with my clients."

People in law schools and legal offices have admitted they don't tell the whole truth to law students. The thinking is that if students really knew what the job is like they wouldn't come into it, so it's better to get them in first and then let them find out later...tragic.

The same blinders-on approach is voiced by people training nurses, police officers, social workers and correctional staff. Their bottom line is not long term performance, it is turning out qualified people.

Honest Education Is Needed

When recruits don't know about the emotional demands of the job there is a painful clash between ideals and reality. Not only do these people feel quickly exhausted, but frustration, disillusionment and anger at the situation and themselves take a priceless toll. For hundreds of thousands of nurses, social workers, police officers and other helpers, things are not turning out the way they were supposed to. And there doesn't seem to be any help.

Too many doctors and nurses modeled their job expectations from Marcus Welby, Medical Centre and other Hollywood visions of health care. Detectives and police officers are weaned into the profession from police shows. Young people become lawyers because it looked so good and sexy on L.A. Law. And the training programs often lead young people further down the path, never bothering to mention it doesn't lead to the pretty garden presented by Hollywood.

Hollywood influences many career choices with exciting dramas in which life's most challenging situations are solved in one hour with six commercial breaks. Many graduates are shocked to discover jobs don't come with commercial breaks.

Students are often misinformed by teachers who may not have worked in the profession, or cared for the troubled or sick, for many years. The ideals the student learns are often unrelated to the real world of staff shortages, under-funding and communication blocks. Nurses are often lured by ads that read, "The hospital that places patients first" or "the hospital that really cares". The young nurse values caring and nurturing, hoping to help people and participate in the healing, but once in the hospital, what she was taught and what she wants to believe clash with reality. Again... training programs are geared directly to getting graduates hired, what happens after that is someone else's responsibility.

In the isolation of the classroom the trainers do not witness the pain, trauma, disillusionment and anger suffered by idealistic, energetic people who believe in their profession and their personal potentials. Trainers do not see the slow erosion of spirit and of hope. They do not see the pills being swallowed, the drinks being gulped, the smoking, the insomnia, the divorces or child abuse.

Teaching Without Terrorizing

Students can be forewarned without being scared off. Equipping people for survival does not need to be negative or frightening. It requires knowledge, honesty and tools for beating burnout.

Not teaching caregivers the tools for beating burnout is a tragic omission in most training programs. A few hours is all that is required to make graduates aware that there are pitfalls. Books like this one can easily offer the tools to sidestep the pitfalls *before* falling.

Police officers, for example, are given thorough training on how to fire a gun but little or no guidance on how to deal with emotional stress. Ironically most officers will never fire their gun on duty but they will all deal repeatedly with emotionally demanding situations.

Prison guards deal with inmates who are frustrated, angry, unsocialized, irrational and often physically threatening. Their training is heavy on security procedures and the use of weapons but rarely does their training include guidance on how to survive their job.

Think about the wasted dollars, wasted time and unnecessary trauma that could be avoided by teaching coping skills to people in helping professions.

Ideals Need To Be Based On Reality

People entering a profession need to be equipped with accurate expectations and tools for coping. As a result there are fewer surprises and reality shocks that shatter their ideals and make them feel like total failures.

Keeping recruits naive may seem to be the easy and efficient way, but in the long run it isn't. Honest information about the realities of the job will result in some people realizing that this is the wrong career for them, and this is preferable. Research indicates the costs associated with attrition and turnover in the workplace can be greatly reduced by teaching realistic previews of the job.

Equipping The Mind And Heart

Prior knowledge about burnout equips people to recognize it in the early stages, either in themselves or in others. They can anticipate the sources of stress ahead of time, going in with a "this isn't going to get me attitude" rather than a "what's happening, why am I feeling this way, I must not be right for this job" attitude.

Professionals are rarely taught interpersonal (communication and caring) skills. Rapport skills are easy to teach and fun to learn. Even a professional who isn't a warm, caring, people person can learn effective rapport skills that leave the communicators feeling satisfied.

A personal friend, Mary Bray, has been Canada's top real estate sales person several years running. She explains her success in a city where housing prices were substantially below major urban centres.

"I've been doing over ten million dollars a year in sales because I take care of people. It doesn't matter what business you are in, take care of your people and the money takes care of itself."

She would spend time with people, get to know them and their likes and find them the best house.

"Many times I talked someone out of buying a house because I knew a better buy would come up. Sometimes they would spend less money but it was a better house for them. Years after putting someone in a good house I get thanked, and they've sent me other people."

Sometimes caring for people requires extra consideration and time, but the extra, *human,* touches are what set you apart and will prevent burnout. When you are appreciated for what you do, you experience fulfillment.

Too often, particularly in medicine, caring for people is considered "small talk". Chatting skills are regarded as pleasant but not essential.

One physician told me "If that's what they want they should go see a priest." This doctor is a burnt out person who can still compute and prescribe but I think he is dangerous, bordering on being an agent for the drug companies that pay for some of his holidays.

Rapport Skills Can Be Taught

Communication and rapport skills can be taught. Too may people believe interpersonal skills are natural "gifts" that some people are just blessed with.

Anyone can be taught rapport skills that open the lines of communication and any trainer can learn these rapport skills through good Neuro Linguisitic Programming courses or through my Discovering Potentials and Beating Burnout courses. Information on courses is available by writing to the address at the back.

Regarding rapport skills as on-the-job training means people are learning a fundamental aspect of their job by trial and error, with the errors being at the client's expense.

The "if it works, keep doing it" approach doesn't mean the best techniques are being used. It's a *get by* attitude that leaves the person wondering if they're doing it right.

When Those In Need Don't Help Themselves

A continuing problem for physicians and caregivers is "patient noncompliance" -a jargony way of saying not following advise. These *"in"* jargony terms are a great part of the problem. All of the professions have developed code words to keep other people in the dark. Listen to politicians who've "interfaced and transferred hard copy communications" to realize that this gobblty gook word game is ridiculous. It blocks the one thing people need most, communication.

If you want someone to help themself communicate to them why your suggestion is worth doing, show them how to do it and before you set them free make sure they understand why doing it is of value to them.

"Do you understand why it is important for you to make this change" is a question I ask. If they aren't sure, I'll sometimes have them close their eyes and see themselves in the future. I have them imagine themself having made the change...see how that looks and feels, see if your life is better through this change. Then I have them look at what their life will be like if they don't change. Invariably they see their life as worse or just the same.

From that point on it is their choice. It is their Life and I let them have it.

The extra ninety seconds it takes to let someone see their Life with the change and without it releases me. If they can't see that this is going to be a benefit they aren't going to do it. "I Love you and set you free" is something I've often affirmed in my mind as people have left my office. I can give them the tools for healing but I can't protect anyone from themself.

Everyone owns a Life path. If the solution I've suggested doesn't feel right to them, we'll try to create another solution. By listening, caring and honoring their intelligence I've learned many tools and techniques. My clients are my greatest teachers.

Organizations And Burnout

Organizations must realize the importance of a person's sense of identity and Self-worth. Organizations must humanize and manage people. Again: *the essence of managing is to give employees what they need to be excellent at what they do.* That means the tools, the education, the motivation, the praise and the creative freedom to find better ways of doing it.

When the employee doesn't feel he or she has an impact on the process, the fire of passion is smothered.

Institutions are dead things. Institutions are not alive, they do not breath, as soon as the people are removed they are fossils. The products of every institution are created by people for people. We must humanize the whole process, the whole environment. We must humanize our society.

All we have to do is look at the architecture of the 70s and early 80s to see what an inhuman time we've been through. The 70s cold boxy buildings were not designed for humanity, they were designed for institutions. They are dehumanizing, intimidating, cold and impersonal. The air is bad and the windows don't open.

"So...we'll see ya at work on Monday?"

The directors of institutions must turn their energies toward people and enhance each workers sense of personal accomplishment, passion and desire to do the job.

If an employee does not feel liked, needed and valued they will not perform. Humanity is an essential need.

Before an organization will become more human, its people must become more human. We must acknowledge the Self. We must like, need, and value SELF before an organization will. Any organization exists <u>because</u> of people, not in spite of people. This is why there is so much hostility between unions and management groups. Management feels the organization survives in spite of the union and unions feel they survive in spite of management. The common goal, humanity, ease and peace are lost and any value of the human work experience is lost. Everyone is just killing time, and that's killing people.

We Need To Know Why We Do What We Do

Organizations must remind employees why they do what they do. They must see the end result occasionally to remember what they are contributing to.

A turkey processing operation was having trouble with personnel so they commissioned me to write a film. The film I wrote reminded the people who process turkeys that those frozen white balls of ice that leave the plant are the centre of North American family traditions. I gave them human images to show that each employee is contributing a worthwhile, healthful and quality product to moms, dads and kids. By reminding the employees that their work is the centre piece of the Norman Rockwell Thanksgiving dinner painting, a renewed sense of purpose swept through the plant.

Government employees who process paper and numbers particularly need to know how they are contributing to the well being of people. If they can't be shown, we've uncovered the problem.

Chapter 10:   False Cures

If you ask yourself each day, what am I afraid of and confront that fear with courage and knowledge, you will always be empowered.

Denial is a way of avoiding fear. It takes courage and honesty to know Life. First you have to admit there is resistance and many people won't do that until their resistance to Life is a disease. If there is stress or pressure I guarantee other people already see the problem and its effects. You're not able to totally hide it.

Once you've identified the resistance you must assess how much of it you've caused. That's probably the hardest part of all, admitting responsibility for your Life. Letting go of the victim mentality and acknowledging that you create your Life experiences, is a major growth experience.

Denial of the problem is the easy way out... for a while. Denial sometimes works because some things, minor upsets, fade away on their own. But the things that really matter, the bigger challenges, don't fade away.

You live within your mind and you create your mind through your interpretations of your experiences. When you don't put your energy into Life it crumbles.

Who To Blame

As Louise Hay teaches in her excellent book, "You Can Heal Your Life" , "blame is one of the surest ways to stay *in* a problem. In blaming another we give away our power."

Blaming other people for how we are is ridiculous. Blaming parents is hogwash. If you can point a finger and identify a cause you can change the effect. You've created yourSelf. In my film "A Journey To The Soul" I teach that your soul is not a piece of your mother's soul or your father's soul, it is distinct and individual, one of a kind created and sustained by you.

The many times your parents were less than perfect and didn't react the way you wanted them to - the times they weren't like the moms and dads on TV, the times parents were weak and confused, stumbling through their own lessons, have no effect on your today, unless you won't take responsibility for your Life.

Parents do the best they can with the understanding, awareness and knowledge they have. If you think your parents are your problem it is time to release the past. If you expect a boss to be the father or mother you never had, you're going to be disappointed.

You don't use yesterday's garbage to make today's meal. Why would you let your childhood dominate your adulthood? You're not a child any more. <u>You</u> are creating your Life. Blaming others doesn't get you what you want or need. It is fearing responsibility for your own change. You don't need a father or a mother now, you need you.

The Lessons Of Humility

People at high risk of burnout are apt to have long range and elaborate plans, ability and high expectations. But Life teaches us humility. When we get greedy we lose what we had. When we get too high and mighty a lesson in humility is just around the corner.

Disappointments and detours are a part of every Life. Lovers stop loving, they ask for divorces and they die; children become alien and rebellious; supervisors stop supporting and start criticizing; bureaucracy stifles positive change and the achievements you feel you've earned. No Life is without surprises, tragedies and disappointments. So why be angry to have had yours?

Your problems are so much more challenging than the problems of other people, aren't they?

Thousands of people have read that last sentence and nodded their heads. Our own problems seem so different from everyone else's.

Everyone has to improvise solutions to every new challenge that comes along. When we've got the solution, it isn't a problem, it's just that old challenge again. We deal with it and move on because we've already learned that lesson.

If it is a problem it means there is something to learn from it. Problem is a heavy, prickly label we apply to Life's next lesson.

The essence of the word problem is probe.

Denial Leads To Disaster

There are only two motivating emotions, Love and fear. If we're loving we stretch and experiment, learn and grow. If we choose fear, we deny, we block and we feel overwhelmed. By denying we become dull and dead. Denial takes many forms, it can be as simple as becoming a television vidiot, abusing food, cigarettes, retreating to bed, then it leads to more serious coping mechanisms like booze, pills and disease.

When we reach for a crutch we're not mustering our strengths for action; we're simply taking flight in a passive manner, hoping ignore-ance will make it go away. At best, denial can blanket the pain for a little while, but it soon stops working, and we require heavier and still heavier armour to protect us.

That's when we venture into the heavy world of False Cures, using any means at hand: drugs, gambling, sex, alcohol, excessive work, sports or games.

A terrible thing happens when we dull or deaden our pain, we deaden our soul. We allow a decaying aspect of our

Life to get worse. We've run from the next lesson Life has to offer, and that lesson can chase us into the ground.

Camouflage Is Not A Cure

If you're camouflaging a problem, it is important to try identifying the source. You're burning out for some reason and if you continue in a state of denial you drop into an abyss.

Beware of phrases like, *there is nothing wrong with me... I can't do anything about the problem... I survived it before... What good would it do to change... Maybe the problem will go away.*

The New Job

In desperation a burnout victim may leave a job and seek another in the hope passion will be kindled. But beginning a new job in a depleted state of great expectation is a set-up for another disaster. The second job could promote burnout even more quickly because the essence of burnout is not the environment as much as an individual's response to the environment. The burned out person is sensitized to negative situations and if the individual doesn't develop positive solutions to reality, they risk a repeat performance, possibly becoming unable to work at all.

Finding Better Ways To Cope

I love my "safe places" where I'm quiet and peaceful and enveloped by Nature. I often go there with a pad and pen.

If you'd like to find a better way to cope go to a quiet place and look at your answer to question 1 in the "How Are You Coping" questionnaire. Lets find out what you don't enjoy about what you are doing, and why don't you enjoy it.

Start by writing:

I don't like

Then finish the sentence as many ways as you honestly can.

After you've written the *don't like* list finish each item by adding the word *because* and then finish the sentence again. For example:

I don't like - the empty feeling I have about work *because* I need to be praised and encouraged.

Go for the essence of the problem now. Let it pour through you, almost as though your hand is doing the thinking. Don't hold back, nobody else needs to see this paper.

After you've done this write what you feel you need. For example:

I don't like - the empty feeling I have about work *because* I need to be praised and encouraged. <u>Encouragement</u>

Underline the things you need. Now do your best to have your needs satisfied. You have legitimate needs, don't be afraid to ask for what you need and begin asking for help, Love and guidance from yourSelf.

It is very likely you've been letting yourSelf down. Look at your list of needs and think of ways you can satisfy them before asking others to. The solution can be as simple as praising yourSelf and celebrating accomplishments.

Let's now think of a couple of people you can talk to. Who can you talk to about work? Someone who would understand the pressures and may have ideas for you to try.

Think of another person you can talk about <u>Life</u> with. This needs to be someone you respect, someone who is wise. You may not know them very well but this is a great way to get to know them. When you approach them be open, you might offer to take them for dinner. Let them know you're looking for some advise. People like to be asked for their opinion and they like to be taken out for dinner, so you'll probably get a positive response, but don't be surprised if they have to fit it into their schedule. Wise friends are in demand.

In Search Of Oz

Look at your answer to question 5 in the "How are you coping" questionnaire. Where would you like to be?

Why would you like to be there? What are the elements or qualities of this place that attract you?

How are you going to get there?

I really believe in satisfying your wants. If you want to be somewhere then get yourself there. If you really feel passionate about it you will be able to go. So go.

If your attitude is, *Well Peter, I mean... I'd like to go but I can't go. I mean, I can't really go there.*

Tell me why you can't go there. Write it down and look at that answer.

You've only got two options. Go to this place and possibly love it, or be happy where you are. If you can't love where you are then leave it. If you can't leave it then love it.

Many people think of a place they had a wonderful vacation. Vacations aren't real. After a while even the most Edenistic places become boring because we need challenges.

There was a time I wanted to be in sunny California. All those movies and television shows made it look so great. People in California really had it together, sunshine, great beaches, beautiful people. They didn't seem to have any problems.

I flew to Los Angeles and as we made our approach to the L.A. airport I saw the Hollywood sign and the tiny palm trees... my heart swelled and I Loved California. Yes I was finally here, in the place I'd dreamed of and it was going to be wonderful.

Then we landed.

Lost luggage, angry travellers, pollution, traffic jams, poverty, dirt.

I had to go there to know that the place I was dreaming of doesn't exist. I like parts of California and I spend a few weeks there speaking and teaching every year, but Life is Life wherever you go. Every place and every situation has challenges to be overcome.

Life is where you are. If you need to run away then arrange to run away. But don't close the doors that you've opened here. Set it up so that you can come back if you want to.

Sex, Drugs and Booze

To know more about sex, booze and drugs look at questions 7, 8 & 9 in the coping questionnaire. Remember situations where you used these devices to feel better. Did it make you feel better?

Think back and remember what was making you feel bad.

Which works best, changing what makes you feel bad or using drugs, booze or sex to numb the hurt for a while?

Did the booze, drugs or sex create a new kind of hurt?

Are two hurts worse than one?

If you want to be less hurt, resolve the cause of the original hurt.

If you can't remember the original hurt and the booze, drugs or sex is out of control isn't it time to get help? Alcoholics Anonymous is available and can connect you with people who can give you the tools to solve the original problems rather than stack them up.

Gaining Control

Control can be gained by looking at your answers to questions 10 & 11 of the Coping questionnaire. Think about any times you've lost control. What were you thinking about when you lost control?

What did you do?

Who did you hurt?

Do you want to continue hurting? If your answer is no then talk to someone who can help you. If you do want to continue hurting then your pain isn't bad enough for you to change. I honor that, but try not to hurt other people. Keep your pain for yourSelf. You're choosing it, so you live with it.

Make a promise to yourself by finishing this sentence. I'll stop this negative behavior when _____.

If a friend finished that sentence the way you did, what would you say to them?

Know What You Really Want

If you're using a coping mechanism like booze, cigarettes, drugs, sex or physical abuse, as you feel the need rising ask yourSelf what you're really needing. What do you really want. Is it Love, is it acceptance, is it change or peace? Peace is only a thought away from anger.

Think of ways you can get more of the real thing in your Life. Go after it, you're worth it. Life is not a dress rehearsal, this is the real thing.

Chapter 11: Personal Solutions

People who are good at Life, who do well at their job, who do well in their friendships, who stay healthy and happy, are the people who know that Life is a celebration of consciousness, to be enjoyed. They know that balance is an important part of living.

You need to fulfill all parts of your Self. You need to know your Self, your needs and desires and to stop frantic, frenetic, obsessive behavior motivated by fear or frustration. In other words, stop abuse and Love yourSelf enough to care for yourSelf.

The denial of personal, human and emotional needs prevents you from being fully functional. If you aren't in touch with Self you're living numb. Inner wisdom, that wise and knowing part of you that sometimes sounds like the little voice of your conscience, is a good voice to start listening to. It may be your spirit or soul talking to you. It may be that child you used to be, full of hopes, dreams and expectation. How is that child? We all carry the child within and if that child is denied the essential elements of Life, the child rebels, shuts the system down and demands the Love and care you deserve.

It amazes me that so many people who feel a lack of Love from a parent continue not to Love themselves.

Through these solutions, we tackle the three major aspects of burnout. We (a) reduce emotional strains (b) offset the negative, depersonalized views of people and Self and (c) boost your tools for control, fulfillment and Self Love.

Each technique requires patience, practice and a bit of courage. Each needs to be adapted so it fits your Life comfortably. I learned long ago that if it isn't comfortable it isn't going to be used.

Not all the suggestions are for all people. Find what works best for you, experiment a bit and play with the ideas, even the crazy sounding ones. You may be surprised at how well they work. If something doesn't appeal to you, ask yourSelf honestly if it is because it tackles the *IT* of the situation. Ask yourSelf if you resist because it means changing the essential part of yourSelf that is hurting.

If the answer is yes, I advise you to put fear aside and move into the state of change. When we react strongly to something, either positively or negatively, it's becausewe recognise something we can learn from.

Embrace Change

If you think of yourSelf as writing a Life story you'd want it to be interesting wouldn't you? You wouldn't want every chapter to begin and end the same way. Each new chapter is an introduction of new situations, new developments, challenges and resolutions.

Each chapter has the potential to be richer and more exciting than the last. It makes sense because you've grown through the past chapter, there is more experience to live with now.

Change is one of the few constants in Life. Just look around and see that everything is changing. Even rocks evolve over the course of time, but their change is almost imperceptible so we don't consider rocks to be alive.

Some people live like a rock.

To stop changing is to cease living. That might help explain why the ability to grow and change through the seasons of Life has a great deal to do with longevity. When we're good at Life, when we love its quirks, quarks and surprises, we get to continue. But when we become angry at Life or disappointed and cold like a stone, the Life energy drains away and the body becomes dust again.

Life is a constant state of change. From the moment we were born nothing has stayed the same; everything is always changing. That's Life! Yet change is something most people fear. We think we want to gather things in place, so we have everything just right, then hang onto that moment so it'll last. But it doesn't, it won't, it can't.

The whole Life plan is a constant state of evolution. You are evolving at this moment. Oliver Wendell Holmes once said, "Man's mind stretched to a new idea, never goes back to its original dimension." Who you are now is different than who you were yesterday.

If you do not allow yourSelf to continue to grow, to learn and develop you will stop changing and stop living. I guarantee it.

People who do not accept that Life is a twisting, turning, surprising roller coaster without a finish line, do not last at Life, they die of resistance.

People who commit suicide refuse to change. They stop flowing with Life and choose denial, anger and resistance rather than change. Many people are in a state of passive suicide, doing little Self destructive things, making little anti Life and anti happiness choices.

Embrace change, try different things, you don't have to do anything the same old way and easing back to the old habits is simple when the old habits were right in the first place. Experimenting with change is to learn something new, or to confirm the value of the old. This moves you from believing to knowing, but there is always room for experimenting.

Stay A Student

You are a passenger on school house Earth. The lessons Life has to offer you aren't over until you leave that body. My personal goal is to be really good at Life, I'm working on a

Ph.D. in Life. Every person and every situation has something to teach us.

Your clients or patients have many things to teach you, and you can learn a tremendous amount by reversing the communication dynamic. Invite your clients to review you. Ask them if they feel satisfied with what you've done for them. You'll find out very quickly what's working and what isn't, and what recipients expect and need.

The early warning sign of burnout - depersonalizing clients as though they aren't human - negates the possibility that these people could teach you something, but they always can.

No two people have had the same Life experiences. No two people are the same, therefore they do not fit into slots. Each person is a wonderful combination of experiences and emotions and my clients are my teachers. Together we discover the solutions that are of the highest good for them.

I Love Life and I Love my clients. I allow them their learning process and I don't burn out.

How could I possibly burn out from meeting wonderful people with challenging questions for me to help them answer? If I've listened, cared and offered what I know failure isn't possible.

Maybe you can find a similar way of viewing Life and your work.

Letting Bitterness Go

We have a fundamental need to forgive and to Love. But our society can teach us that those who forgive and forget are patsies, people who are always victimized or blamed.

People who do not forgive become bitter and very often burn out. A grudge is a nasty, thorny thing to hang on to.

Bitterness results from several situations.

1. Negative motives or jealousy: People who compare, feel weak and envy the abilities of others.

2. Negative reactions to challenges: In its simplest form this is conditional love. The marketing of the emotion love is a popular tragedy resulting in the attitude *I give you my love as long as you give me your love the way I think it should be given*. This type of conditional love produces disappointment, harshness and bitterness. How can someone else know how you want to be loved all the time when you don't know yourSelf? Have you always loved yourSelf?

3. Negative responses to Life's learning opportunities: The positive response requires you to choose peace, to go within and ask your inner wisdom for the response that is of the highest good. It is to search for the lessons in all things, knowing that often what we perceive to be a setback turns out to be a boost.

4. Choosing anger and hate: Do you feel you can't forgive? To be more honest replace the word can't with won't. "I won't forgive". Forgiveness is like Love, it is a choice involving an act of will.

Frequently bitterness is fertilized by choosing to remember, to dwell on and talk about offenses that have occurred. We voice our pain to anyone who will listen and even those who would rather not. The quiet moments are spent stewing in a painful past rather than meditating on the potentials of the future. What person's past does not include pain?

Anyone who does not hope for a better future burns out.

Releasing The Past

All trauma is followed by a period of adjustment. A facet of your Life has been dramatically altered or voided. You need to relearn living, to peacefully heal and refill that void through a new situation and it is important to give emotions time to heal. It is vital that you feel emotions, that you feel the seasons of your Life and know that to sense the emptiness is also to appreciate the possibility of fullness. To feel sad is not to be failing at Life, it is to be very essentially alive.

Our society may teach us to think that if we're not happy, we're not succeeding. But there is a rainbow of emotions. In every Life there are seasons, some of joy and laughter, others of pain and sorrow. In my film 'A Journey To The Soul' I talk about an 82-year-old woman who changed my perception of Life.

In my early 20s I remember being a network television reporter in New Brunswick Canada and I'd been assigned to interview her. She had just received the order of Canada award from our Prime Minister.

This woman had never been more than thirty miles from her modest home set in a pine forest. She had been a midwife, and had delivered most of the people living in her sixty mile world.

She was funny, wise and the most beautiful person I've ever met. She glowed and her eyes shone and twinkled and her light filled that little white farm house.

She told me stories of her Life, her Loves and losses. Four of her ten children and three husbands had died. Yet she was filled with Life.

I asked her why she wasn't sad as she told the stories of her losses and she smiled and looked deep into my eyes.

"Every life has joys and sorrows." she said. "Why would I be sad to have had mine?"

She was 82 years old and more alive than most people I've known. She had mourned and grieved but she didn't hold a grudge against Life, she forgave Life and continued to celebrate it.

"This is Life", she said holding her hands out to encompass totality. "Be good at it."

You are alive, feeling, caring. To block feelings is to block Life energy. You may think you put up a front but, as explained in chapter one, the emotions will fester, create energy blocks, dis-ease and bring you to your knees. Think about it. Might your burnout be emotional burnout, an implosion activated by your resistance to feeling or grieving?

It may be that you have welled up tears that need to come out. The child within may need to cry because of a hurt your adult Self denied.

I encounter many people, particularly men, who are emotionally blocked. The symptoms can be anything from alcoholism to tension, to wife abuse, to child abuse. These are only symptoms, I want to resolve the cause. Using hypnosis I interview their subconscious. I say "at the count of 3 we will go back to the time when the seed of the problem was planted."

I never know the sensitizing event but their subconscious does. It takes us back to one, two maybe ten events.

Again and again sensitizing events happen between the ages of five and thirteen. These captains of industry, lawyers, politicians, will remember and allow the emotions to flow. Then we go through a forgiveness process and through processes like the two described below. Information on my forgiveness tape program is at the back of the book.

Burnout: a sane reaction to insanity

Getting from one end of a career to the other can be like walking a path dotted with land mines. Burnout is common when a society does not nurture and support an individual.

Today the Self aware person might look around and wonder "What kind of society have I committed myself to. "

We live in a society in which the two greatest thrusts of science are Medicine, the science of prolonging human Life even when the body's organs are shutting down, and the science of War. The science of mass suicide.

The World is O.K., Nature and the Cosmos are O.K., but society...not as O.K. as when it was more in touch with humanity. Affluence and technology are not solutions for Life's worthwhile questions.

We can all recognize the social burnout around us and in such an atmosphere of dehumanization you might have a tendancy to put a thicker shell around yourSelf. But isolation is not the answer. We are gregarious creatures with a need for tradition, rituals and banding together.

Shutting yourself away may be necessary to find and heal yourSelf, to know the world within you, but don't lock the door so no one else can come in.

Closeness Is A Cure

We can spare ourselves tremendous agony and turn our lives around by cultivating closeness. Where there is communication, caring and bonding, burnout has a hard time staking claim.

Society is an alienating experience making closeness scarce as lives become more and more fragmented. We must actively seek out closeness and work at it.

It starts with becoming close with yourSelf. The values exercise lets you know what you really value. It can lead you to Self.

By giving yourSelf what you need you can rediscover what a good, caring person you can be, not the loathsome creature that has to be hidden away, covered over or given three coats of paint before being trotted out for the public.

To feel closeness take yourself out in Nature, to a beach or a park or a forest, some beautiful place away from people. Spend four hours walking and sitting and lying and thinking and looking. Think about the sky and trees and Earth. Think the things you used to think as a child exploring this amazing planet.

To establish closeness with ourSelf and other people we have to be willing to take chances. The two barriers to closeness are not talking and not listening. True listening requires some effort. It means making a conscious effort to hear, paying close attention to what is being communicated verbally and physically. True listening means listening with the ears, the eyes, the mind and the heart.

If we want to have a friend, we must be a friend. Be the type of person you would like to be with, caring, open compassionate, encouraging, forgiving and loving and see what comes back to you.

If you take yourself too seriously you'll always be on the lookout for opportunities to justify what you did or why you did it. You'll miss Now agonizing over the past.

Being defensive never works. When you are right you don't have to defend yourself and if you're wrong you can't.

The ability to laugh at some dumb thing you've done is a great step toward your humanity. The ability to laugh at yourSelf makes Life a lot less painful. Humans have foibles, we make boo boos and there is nothing wrong with being wrong. Being wrong is O.K. because recognizing it moves you to being more right.

We needn't be embarrassed to be in the wrong, it is simple to appreciate the lesson and acknowledge that we're wiser now than before. Life as a student of everything is healing and a lot more fun.

A social position, heritage, title or qualification that makes you think you are special can be a handicap. Specialness comes from within. We all have birthright gifts we can choose to develop. Specialness is an awareness from within, not a title imposed on the outside. Royalty, heirs, people who are born priveledged can be painfully unaware and without purpose. People who squat on a job title thinking they deserve respect are buffoons. They become a prisoner of ego.

I choose to be a student of everything rather than a frightened man clinging to ego.

Release Your Perception Of Status

Enlightenment comes from listening, admitting imperfection, allowing other points of view, releasing yourSelf from position or status and letting people get close to you. No one has so much status that they can get through Life alone. It is only lonely at the top when you believe that is where you are.

To let the barriers down we need to identify the barriers we've erected. Check yourSelf and see if you trust others or if you're afraid. Shyness is a fear of being rejected. When was the last time you confided something you considered crucial to someone else? Can you really listen and care about someone else over the long term? Can you feel calm responding to a point of view different than your own? Can you laugh at yourSelf? Think back to specific incidents when you failed yourSelf and create ways to do it better the next time.

Look at the relationships in your Life to see if they have trust and depth or if they are of the surface variety. Loving, trusting and knowing requires risking.

The Lesson Of Letting Go

How much are you holding on to? Make a fist now. Squeeze it tightly as though you're holding on. Think of something you're holding on to. How does it feel? Are you straining? How long before it becomes uncomfortable?

As you release the tightness, imagine you're letting go of whatever it is you've been clinging to. How does it feel to let it go? Does it feel natural, easy, better?

The past does not exist anywhere but your mind. If the past is painful then release it and the pain, forgive the past for the lessons you've been offered and let it go.

A grudge is a prickly, thorny thing to hold onto. Anger, fear and regret are not worthy of you, let them go.

Thoughts are things. Feelings and emotions are things and we need to explore them in order to heal. But there comes a time to let the past go, to move into the next chapter, the new season. Stay with the emotions as long as you need to, but know that in time you must let go of the past and grow. Forgive Life for always moving forward, for being so interesting, forgive, pick yourself up and move forward.

To stay the same or hold onto a grudge is to resist Life, to be angry with the whole Life plan. That is a lot to be angry at.

Putting Pain And Anger In Storage

Through my own resistance to letting go of an intense relationship, I began to imagine a U-haul truck backed up to the front of my mind. I took all the painful thoughts, pictures and feelings left over from the relationship and put them into the U-haul.

I'd mourned long enough, there was nothing left to feel or resolve except a prolonged pain, so I let it go into the back of the truck. It was a big truck. When I'd emptied mySelf of these tender thoughts and painful memories I closed the door on the truck and let it drive away to a Cosmic storage place.

If I want those thoughts or memories back I can have the U-haul bring them out of storage, but putting them in a place outside mySelf made a tremendous difference. I still feel pangs of hurt on occasion. I was at a party and my lost love arrived as someone else's date. That gave me some new pictures, thoughts and feelings to deal with. I did, they're now in Cosmic storage too.

Someone who knew the situation asked if it was a drain to see my love with someone else. "No", I said "It wasn't a drain, it was a sewer."

Once you've worked the situation through, done whatever you need to do with it, the Cosmic U-haul is available.

Live In The Now

The past doesn't exist any more, you can't get it back. The past is a cancelled cheque and the future is a promisary note, it isn't here yet, so the only moment you have any real influence on is the present one. If you have a stressful situation stop, ask yourSelf what you can do about it Now. What response can set things right. NOW is the only time you have control of, the only time you will ever control. A moment spent regretting the past or worrying about the future is lost.

Sometimes the time to act is upon you but 80% of the time the situation will resolve itself without your involvement. Often it isn't your problem and the people involved will resolve it. Often the time for action isn't now. If no decision is available, affirm that you require a decision, you've programmed your subconscious so relax, the decision will be received by your conscious mind when it is ready and you are relaxed. Affirm in your mind that when the time is right you accept the solution. Then let it go. When the time for deciding is upon you no decision will be required, you will simply know.

Get A Life

What are you besides a job title? Make a list of the other aspects of your Life. If it is an interesting list you have a balanced Life. If it is a short list, add some things that you'd like to become and become them.

There is more to Life than work. The root of the word business is busy-ness. What is your busy-ness? The word business comes from a time when people had a Life and some busy-ness on the side. Busy-ness was selling extra eggs, selling sewing, trading and marketing. People of the agricultural era did not burn out because they were occupied with survival. Survival is about Life, truth and reality. Our technocratic lives don't focus on Truth or Nature. Very little of an urban life deals with real Life issues.

Don't let your busy-ness destroy your Life. You are not a human doing, you are a human Being.

When your world is work, you have a very narrow, fickle base...easy to fall off of. Your sense of competence, self-esteem and personal identity are on shaky ground. You need a private life to balance the professional one.

Get a Life by setting up clear boundaries between work and play, job and home. When you leave the job, leave it physically and psychologically.

In one of my burnout seminars a lawyer wrote the question, "Why do I bring work home every night but 70% of the time I'm too tired to do it. And why do I look forward to weekends and not to the work weeks?

There are several reasons why he may bring work home. It looks good going out the office door with a brief case of work, good students and grownups do their homework, the day is out of control and night is the only time to get work done, or there may be a problem at home. If home is so empty that you only feel secure with work, then change what's happening at home.

The second part of his question is beautiful because the weekend is the only time he relaxes and allows himself to be off work. I told him to allow himself to be off work every night and to only bring the work home that absolutely has to be done that night.

Your private time gets polluted by work every time you, rehash the day's problems at home, take work home, work overtime, are "on call". Obviously there are times it is necessary to talk about work or bring work home. Accept overtime, but set limits and times when you DO NOT work. Keep these times absolutely for yourself. Your work will always make increasing demands on you, there will always be something more you could do, employers take all they can possibly get. Employers burn people out. Society, mortgages, stuff and greed will burn people out.

Be In Positive Situations

Fun experiences with healthy, happy, active people free of major problems, is an important antidote to negativity. We need to know what wellness and joy feel like. Some people coach a baseball team, work at a summer camp for kids, act in amateur theatre, join a rowing team. The possibilities are limitless. If we aren't around positive people we lose sight of the goals we're working for.

Do You React Or Respond?

My friend Linda Cox teaches people to respond to Life rather than react. When we react it is often from a position of ego. Our reactions are often knee jerk and regrettable.

Responding to a situation means realizing that you are best when you are relaxed and flowing. Saying the word *respond* to yourSelf reminds you of the choices you have, choices to get involved or pull back, to respond now or to wait for things to settle. You'll live with wisdom and avoid conflict when you respond.

Learning To See The Positive

We tend to be very good at seeing the negative in Life society and particularly in ourselves. Seeing good isn't as easy when we've been conditioned to see bad.

As children we're often taught to compare, to compete, to critique. The education system focuses on weakness. The grades that aren't good are the ones that get attention and discussion. As a result we can lose our birthright gifts, the natural gifts and talents we're born with.

If a child is good at art and creative work but isn't good at math and science that child is told to put the art aside and concentrate on the math and science.

The child does this, raises the math and science marks and a big fuss is made over the accomplishment. Lots of praise and pats on the back.

Tragically, what many children do is concentrate on the math and science, looking for the praise and achievement through struggle, and abandon the birthright gifts, the talents that came naturally were not honored.

Insight can come from pictures of yourself as a child, look at who you were then and remember what you were naturally good at. There is a lot of information in old photos.

They

I did a private session with a woman who works in the offices of the Cancer Society. Dianne is an enthusiastic worker who likes being in this organization. Because her mother had been challenged by cancer, she believes in the mission of the organization.

Dianne has been shoved from job to job, forced to work in a cold damp corner of a basement at a tiny desk with substandard equipment. She has been pushed around and financially "shafted" for years.

Her supervisors have given her very little respect and taken the attitude that if there is a "dirty job" give it to Dianne.

"They put me into a word processing job which is supposed to pay four dollars more an hour and they gave me a 42 cent an hour increase...They didn't increase my pay properly and they didn't give me any thanks for giving up the job I liked more."

She was transcribing dictated notes from doctors who mumbled and "they would get angry at me because I had to guess at what they were saying."

Dianne was burnt out. She came to me feeling demoralized, depressed and quite abused.

With me she learned to say no, and that she didn't need that job enough to be abused. For five long years she had suffered abuse because "they" knew she needed the job. She had told them she couldn't quit and set herself up for abuse.

Some of the things that were done to her were cruel but they happened and continued to happen because Dianne let it happen. Her Self respect was so low that she couldn't say no.

Other women who'd been in the organization only a few months were turning down dirty jobs that were being handed on to Dianne, who'd been there five years.

"They" came and told her her hours would be changing. She didn't want the new hours because it meant fighting rush hour traffic both ways. She remembered what I told her, and said "No". She said she would quit before taking those hours. Everyone was surprised, including Dianne.

"They" agreed not to change her hours. Dianne is a good worker, she has paid her dues and deserves respect. Now that she knows it she gets it.

Learning to say no, learning to Love and respect her Self turned Dianne's Life and career around. She feels better, looks better, now has her own office, a pay raise and is respected.

They will take whatever *they* can get. *They* will burn you out and then say it was your fault. In most cases it was. We allow other people to do things to us. Often the most honest and dedicated workers are the most abused. They're more dedicated to the illusion of a job than they are to themSelf.

Love yourSelf enough to say no and you may discover you're worth quite a bit to your employer.

Ending Headaches

Burnout often communicates its presence through headaches. It is the mind telling you you've accepted too much pressure at one time. We need to spread our challenges out, not pile them up. Try thinking two thoughts a one time.

We can't do it. Just like we aren't good at doing three jobs at the same time. We do things best one at a time.

Here is the way to beat headaches. Respond at the first awareness of pressure.

1. Close your eyes. Turn them slightly upwards and think of a yardstick standing upright with the number 36 at the top and the number one at the bottom. There are arrows or indicators along the sides of this yard stick and these arrows are attached to your level of relaxation. Allow the arrows to move smoothly and comfortably down to about fifteen.

2. Remain at this level for about two minutes, enjoying the feeling of relaxation.

3. Move your consciousness to the area that registers pain. Become aware of the size, shape and colour of the area.

4. Seek the source of the pain. It may come as a picture, a sound, a thought or a feeling.

5. If you've identified the source seek a solution from your inner wisdom. If no solution comes then release it for a later time. Send all thoughts and feelings associated with it out of your mind. You may think of yourSelf boxing it up and sending it away.

6. Once the problem or feelings have been expelled, imagine a tap installed on one side of the pressure area and open the tap. Allow the pressure and color to drain away counting it down from ten to zero , knowing that with each number the pressure is less and less. You can say it 10 - less pressure, 9 - the pressure is draining away, 8 - draining away,

7 - I'm releasing the pressure, 6 - less pressure... and so on down to zero.

7. Stay in the relaxed state of mind for a few minutes, affirming that when you allow those arrows to move back up to 36 you will not assume the pressure again, you will stay relaxed and resist all pressures, floating through the rest of the day allowing other people to get upset if they choose, but you choose peace.

8. Allow the arrows to move back up to 36 whenever you are ready.

What I've just outlined is the essence of self hypnosis, and many other mind control techniques.

Beating The Blahs

The morning blahs can feel like not wanting to start the day, lethargy, an avoidance of movement. You're fighting against yourSelf. Blahs surface as the two cups of coffee needed to face the day, an hour of procrastinating before starting to work. It can be a lack of desire to speak to anyone or a desire to speak to everyone rather than work. When you begin the day with morning doldrums you infect others. When you generate vim and enthusiasm you're a motivator.

The first step to overcoming morning blahs is to realize that you are in control, that you've created your behavior and if you don't like it you can change it. You've been putting up with this morning behavior for how long?

Is it time to let it go?

Here is a simple and extremely effective technique. It is also a little bizarre if you don't understand mental anchors and the workings of the thymus gland.

Mental anchors are associations that you've established. For instance most of us have a mental anchor linking feelings of approval and being Loved with a hug. When we're hugged we register approval from others and ourSelf. You've been taught a hug means approval but you could also have been taught that a kick in the pants means approval. Other cultures have other anchors that trigger specific responses.

I'm teaching you to set up a new morning anchor.

This is a particularly good anchor because it stimulates the thymus, a gland located in the chest where the breast plate meets the throat. If you take three fingers and thump on the breast plate you vibrate and activate the thymus gland just behind it.

Tapping the thymus will stimulate an energy response.

Here is the technique. In the morning take a minute to relax, smile and tap on your thymus gland. I know it sounds strange but try it. The smiling is very important because just as your emotions register through your body, your body positions influence your emotions.

Any time you want to feel emotionally strong take the posture of feeling and being strong and your emotions follow. Looking up is relaxing and results in a smile.

Here is the ultimate kicker for beating the blahs. When you are feeling content or happy in a situation or with people you enjoy, give your thymus gland a little tap. I find myself doing this automatically now and I have a total physical and emotional anchor for putting myself into an optimistic and power state of mind.

As you fall asleep you can program yourSelf for feeling up and energized in the morning. Make this the last thing you say to yourSelf, *I will awaken feeling refreshed and when I smile and tap my thymus gland my spirits, energy and attitude will soar.*

Try it, it works!

Your mind controls your perceptions and your body. Take control of your mind. Relax, program yourSelf for what you want and allow yourSelf to have it.

Once you've established this anchor you can use it at any time of the day or night to say bye bye blahs.

Who Are You?

Mirrors can be an enemy or a friend. If you believe you are your body the mirror will turn against you. Guarenteed, your body will age and weaken, but your soul does not. If you remember you are not a human having a spiritual experience you are a spirit having a human experience you'll have a better perspective on your Self.

To make the mirror a friend again, make a list of ten good things about you. Ten of your best qualities. Then take a mirror and set it in front of a window, in natural light, and tell yourself those ten good things.

You may see your SELF for the first time. That laughing, animated person you see is the real you. The stone face you've been showing yourself under the bathroom light bulb, that isn't you, that's your corpse. You are the Life within your body. You are spirit embodied in flesh and that spirit is the essence of you.

It is your spirit that is burning out due to a lack of Love, Love that spirit and nurture that spirit. Give yourSelf whatever you need to be you again.

Just as we need to sleep in order to know we are awake, in each Life time something must die in order for us to live. Each person experiences death during Life in order to know they are alive. In each Life there is a time when awareness of Life dies, when the spirit burns out, when Love is extinguished. This is necessary for a soul to free itself from the cages gravity creates. As my friend Wayne Dyer teaches in his book "You'll

See It When You Believe It". To escape from your cage you must die while you are alive.

One of my best friends motivated me to write this book. He has done the work of three people, a government job, a garden business and maintaining all aspects of a farm.

He hated his job and nine months ago in casual conversation, told me his job was killing him. He was staying in the job only for the money and pension and had sixteen more years before retiring.

As I write this he is recovering from a very serious case of double pneumonia. Due to the dis-ease he has aged thirty years in one year.

We all build cages for ourselves and if we don't learn to listen to our inner wisdom, follow our true values and say no to things we do not want, we stay trapped within our cage.

Burnout takes many forms because our inner wisdom is very creative in the ways it will free us from our cage.

But tragically many people succumb to death before they will succumb to freedom.

Many among us will have to totally burn out before they'll stop competing, stop shouting, stop hating, stop rushing, stop the hurting and re-embrace Life.

There is great wisdom in the simplest things.

Row row row your boat

Gently down the stream

Merrily, merrily, merrily, merrily

Life is but a dream.

Your boat, to be rowed **gently**, not up the stream but **down the stream**. How? **Merrily**. Because Life is the **dream**.

Chapter 12:   Work Solutions

There are only five states of human performance.

1. **Peak Performance**. We are alive, energized, full of energy and optimism, not drained at the end of the day. We feel nurtured and turned on by what we're doing and who we are. Life is good.

2. **Balance**. We're doing O.K., coping well, active, optimistic and in touch with the Self. We may feel tired at the end of the day but it is a good tired, a satisfied tired, and we're able to rebound without any difficulty.

3. **Strain**. We're managing, but keeping it together is draining. We're too busy to organize. Everything feels like hard work so some worthwhile things don't get done. At the end of the day we're aware something isn't right and it's getting more and more difficult to get up for the next day.

4. **Burnout**. We're barely functioning, like a run down clock that's losing time. We can't find the key to wind yourSelves up. We have trouble concentrating, feeling, realizing anything. We give and give and give, exhausted at the end of the day. It's difficult not to be cynical or negative. We're about to break down.

5. **Breakdown**. The body has quit, broken down. It's stopped functioning at any level that allows us to continue. We're disabled, hospitalized and need extensive physical, emotional and spiritual healing. The child within weeps. It is time to relearn Life.

When we're good at Life,
everything else falls into place.

When Life offers an unexpected lesson we can drop into the state of strain, for good reason. We're faced with a new situation that requires thought and creativity. We may need to recreate ourSelf yet again. Moving from strain to balance requires Self nurturing, some honesty awareness and constructive approaches, not negative coping mechanisms.

Alcohol, drugs, shutting people out, denial, abuse are detrimental reactions to a situation that calls for loving yourSelf.

Three Organizational Approaches

This book is for the individual who is battling burnout, but I've outlined two organizational approaches I discuss with management groups.

Support Groups

Through support groups that meet regularly employees can share thoughts so feelings of having no impact, no voice, dissolve away. Ideally there are meetings with and without management. Very often agendas are set in the no management meetings, an employee who is burning out can get help and advice from peers.

Support groups generally happen on a monthly basis, but if there are hot issues to be resolved, the meetings might take place every two weeks. They work best as a casual gathering. It must not become a bitch session, positive resolutions are the goal. (See how not to sabotage your support system)

Downshifting

Downshifting is lightening the load on the bad days. It means doing something less challenging, less emotional and stressful while someone else takes over the heavy load.

Downshifting is working well in hospitals. If a nurse is having a rough day she can downshift and allow someone else to work directly with the challenging patients.

There are days when people don't have as much to give and everyone is better off if they don't try to over give. This requires a bit of team work but it is always well accepted and worth it.

Lateral Movements

CAP is an innovative program increasing productivity and reducing burnout for government operations of Statistics Canada.

Cap works by moving employees laterally to other departments for temporary assignments. The program director responds to employees looking for a change and places them in departments in need of new blood. The assignments can last from a few months to two years.

The employees aren't officially transferred to other departments, they remain employees of the "home" division, continuing to receive the same pay and benefits with a guarantee the home job will be there on completing the CAP assignment.

More than 90 per cent of assignees in Statistics Canada have rated the six year old program "very beneficial".

Personal Changes On The Job

Change is Refreshing

Variety is not the spice; it is the essence of Life. When we feel helpless, trapped, in a rut, powerless - burnout is likely to set in. Helplessness feeds the twin demons of anger and depression. We're starved of energy, emotionally exhausted and hostile. To climb out of the rut do things differently. Allow yourself the refreshment of change. Take more creative control of your day.

There are several ways to do anything. Even varying the order of doing things gives a lift. Try a new way of getting to work, a new way of dressing. Even such simple things as answering the phone or greeting people in new ways can help.

Some things are not very changeable, certain institutional rules for example, but you can change and improve the little aspects of the job. Focus on what can be modified, reshuffle your order of doing things, break things up so there is more variety, try explaining things to people in a more creative way, how can you appeal to their visual sense? How can you inject more Self into the work? If you turn personality off when working then you aren't working, some robot clone is working. Look for opportunities to laugh and to play your way through the day. A kind word and a smile on every face is beautiful. Spread your inner beauty around.

Start by changing little things, then you're in a better position to change bigger things.

Why Isn't Everyone Burning Out?

Why is it that some people become depleted of energy and others in the same situation flow right along? What are they doing to survive? You can find out.

I know a bus driver who has been driving the same route for years. He sees the same people every day at the same time and he takes them the same places every week day. He shows no sign what so ever of burnout. I asked him why.

"I love my job. You may think I'm just a bus driver but I'm a lot more than that. You see that older lady over there, I'm the son she never had. See the fella with the hat on, I'm a friend that he can count on. You see, I'm not a bus driver, I'm a person. I like people and I'm talking to people and hearing about their life and problems all day long. Hey I'm a therapist too! Ha! I think people burn out cause they leave their personality at home every day. I'm me! And I think the Creator intended for me to be me. I tell jokes and talk about things with people and their faces just light up. I'm an important person because I can make people smile. And that makes me smile."

It is true, anyone can make people smile, can make people feel better about themselves. Doing things with a positive attitude, a people attitude, reminds you of your freedoms, and abilities to create, recreate and change things. Don't be surprised when you resolve a long-standing frustration by humanizing the experience.

The Value Of Human Contact

People can burn out because they give their work more than they receive: they give more in effort, caring and energy in helping other people than they receive in appreciation. Dentists are the classic example. They work in offices without anyone to provide either technical appreciation or technical challenge. Many people in a private dental practice have this challenge.

The likelihood of getting negative feedback rather than praise is built into service professions but it is particularly painful for private practitioners who don't have anyone to say, "you did a great job".

There are two solutions to this. The obvious one is for private practitioners, supervisors and directors of organizations to form friendships or support groups with people who do the same work. This contact needs to be positive and creative, not a moaning session. The goal is to generate new ideas for growth on the job. The peers can share triumphs, give and receive feedback, solace and compassion.

Although the "lone wolf" image may be attractive, it leads to burnout. If the Lone Ranger was still riding the range only heigh-hoing Silver, he'd probably be burnt out.

How Not To Sabotage A Support System

Few people have a nurturing support system of like minded professionals and it is one of the most effective ways of beating burnout. Often professionals sabotage their relationships with other professionals. This happens for the following reasons.

When there is a problem we look for the cause. We tend to blame our own problems on the environment, outside influences we don't control. We tend to see other people's problems as their fault. A situation created by their attitude, lack of ability or laziness.

Our degree of respect and a multitude of other personality factors determines the type of cause we will identify. Once you've criticized a colleague in a negative way, pointing the finger at them, you've sabotaged the support system.

Problems can be caused by situations, staff, and circumstances. Other people's feelings are as tender as your own, if someone is asking for help they are not asking for criticism.

The best way to help another person is not to make statements. Ask good questions. Ask them questions you would be asking yourSelf and together find a solution. A "know it all" attitude doesn't come from security, it comes from insecurity.

Everyone is capable of behaving stupidly, intelligently, gracefully, clumsily, gently or harshly. If we are treated as a graceful person we will be more graceful. If we are treated like an idiot we will be less intelligent than if we were treated with respect.

Similarly, our impressions of a person may be one dimensional, based on an isolated incident, a piece of gossip that may be totally untrue. It is important not to judge a person, dismiss a person or write a person off because they are not perfect. I suspect that if any of us reached a prolonged state of perfection, we'd vaporize. This is school house Earth, if you haven't graduated on to a better place, you too still have lessons to learn.

Be a teacher, a lover, not a judge.

Humanize Your Professional Self

Dentists have high burnout because they aren't appreciated or praised for their work. Dentists most often react to this by taking on more patients, but the most successful way for them to deal with burnout is to spend more personal time with each patient. This time can be spent putting patients at ease, reducing anxiety and allowing personalities to emerge. The dentist becomes a three dimensional person and the interaction is much more fulfilling for both dentist and patient.

Dentists, when asked to describe their most typical patients, used words like "sullen", "uncommunicative", "uninteresting", "uninterested". Of course that's how most of us are in a professional's office. We're not the warm, charming, effervescent people our friends know and love. We're generally uneasy, anxious, in a hurry to get it over with.

Rapport skills work. Communication and humanity is irresistible when it is genuine. As the professional becomes more human so does the client. If the professional communicates a real interest in the person and making the experience a pleasant, human one, recipients are in a position to show genuine appreciation - the very thing many helping professionals lack.

Try asking people about what is right in their Life rather than just dealing with what we think is wrong. Develop your abilities to see interesting aspects of people. Grooming, clothing, accents, names, jobs, their ideas about issues are interesting. If you want to be an interesting person, you just have to be interested.

Every person is unique and has something special to offer, if we take the trouble to look for it. Dentists don't work with teeth, they work with people. Teeth can be boring but every person needs a different kind of reassurance, treatment, conversation, as a result each appointment becomes a unique experience. The professional can be refreshed by complimenting different facets of him or her Self.

Spending that little extra human time takes care of everyone. If you take care of people business takes care of itself.

Identify The Legitimate Pressures

It helps to identify the experiences that cause stress and pressure reactions. Take a piece of paper and list your involvements, work, family, volunteering, what ever you are active in.

A university professor made the following list of work demands.

- being an interesting and entertaining lecturer
- advising dozens of students about courses and careers

- appearing to know a lot
- doing a lot of research
- publishing research
- training students to research
- helping colleagues
- serving on many university committees
- impressing people with my broad knowledge
- being the life of the party at faculty functions

Make the lists for work, home and other involvements and then decide which are important, legitimate, reasonable and in your best interests.

Several things happen with this exercise. You discover things to let go of. You may realize that involvements you've been resenting don't place many demands on you. The resentment may be a result of another area of your Life. If you want to be with your family but work won't allow it, don't resent your family.

"No Billy, I don't agree all yuppies are burnouts."

Many of the demands are Self imposed rather than system imposed. You may be making demands far in excess of what your employer expects. The professor's belief he has to be the life of the party is entirely Self imposed. It is important to recognize real demands and imaginary demands.

Eliminate Frustrations

Popping flash bulbs at a concert can be very difficult for a performer. You might have heard stories of celebrities stopping a show because someone was taking photos with a flash. The whole momentum and celebration comes to a halt while the performer asserts control and deals with this source of frustration.

Singer Neil Diamond is a pro. He doesn't like the popping flashes but he understands that some people want to take pictures, he acknowledges human nature and lets his fans blast away with camera flashes during one, and only one, early song in his concerts. He creates a win/win situation. He knows where to place his eyes so he isn't blinded. He doesn't move near the edge of the stage so he won't fall off and the fans are satisfied.

A school teacher who was constantly frustrated with the need to sharpen pencils at the most inappropriate times during a lesson used the same resolution. The beginning of the lesson, when things were still settling down, was designated pencil sharpening time. Problem solved.

If something frustrates you how can it be creatively resolved? Write down your biggest frustrations and think about cures for the situation. By healing the frustrations you heal yourSelf.

Set Realistic Goals

Professional helpers often have high ideals - fighting injustice, making the world a better place, bringing health and happiness to all, and so on. Idealism can be great, but idealists often become cynics. Ideals are very abstract, they're about vague and sometimes unrealistic goals that aren't real and virtually impossible to maintain in this society. Things are the way they are, not for one reason but for a thousand reasons.

For every action there is an equal and opposite reaction. The way society is, is a result of many forces. Yes, there is room for improvement, but if an ideal or dream is costing you happiness, if it's obsessive, you're heading for four alarm burnout. In my next book on burnout I'll be writing about people who have to 'save the world' and the pitfalls of being a messiah.

Here is a great exercise I share in beating burnout seminars. **Stop all critical thinking and statements** for two days. This isn't easy. You may discover that you've been very hard on this world and hard on yourself. Try it - stop all critical thinking and see how much easier you are to live with.

Set Your Own Pace

Whenever I feel pressure or stress, my relaxation response kicks in. The instant I feel pressure I say "relaxation" to mySelf. We're much better at everything relaxed. Often when I'm being interviewed on television or radio the interviewer sets a pace and fires the questions, sometimes trying to trip me up. Some people think this is entertaining, I don't because the wrong information can come out.

We are best at communicating when we are relaxed. Once the question has been asked, whether it is a work performance review or a network television interview, the questioner is obliged to wait for the answer. I make them wait for the correct answer because I believe that's what they want.

Don't be bamboozled by someone else who sets a frantic pace. You're not good frantic and neither are they. Help them learn that relaxed is better.

When I hosted my own television interview show in Toronto I learned "I don't know" is a good answer. It is a refreshing and honest answer and it relieves us of a lot of pressure. Don't think you have to know everything about a subject.

We Can't Save People From Themselves

Everyone is doing the best with what they have to work with. We always do our best, so there is no point in becoming angry or placing blame on anyone, including yourSelf. Self does not lead us astray but roles, jobs and fear do.

From time to time, we meet someone who is banging their head against a wall. Caregivers deal with these people every day. We see people doing Self destructive things and wondering what's going wrong. They'll stand and bang their heads into their problem until their head aches and they can't think straight any more. All we can do is lead them to the solutions we know can work.

That is all you can do for anyone. Then you must stand back and allow them to use the door. And time and time again they will look at you, walk back to their wall and bang...bang...bang.

Did you fail? Is it right to feel powerless and weak? Heck no! You showed them the door but they weren't ready to use it.

Human Nature: It has to get bad enough before we'll stop, allow our Self to learn the better way and make it better.

I learned this a long time ago. The pain has to be bad enough for us to want to change. And sometimes we need to take ourselves all the way down before we'll decide to change. It's human nature. If we drag someone through the door they probably won't stay there very long before finding something else to bang their head against.

As a therapist who works with Cancer and AIDS patients I know that I can't save them from their own dis-ease. But I may be able to teach them how to find the cause of dis-ease, how to become more comfortable, how to actively choose Life or how to accept their transition into death.

To be successful all I have to do is be a teacher, to show them how to be less anxious, more comfortable and more communicative with themselves and with others. I do not control their illness and I do not carry responsibility for their Life.

Everyone is dealing with something. Everyone is learning a lesson about Life. Allow people their learning process. Be a good teacher, be a care giver, be a forgiver but do not be a saviour. We cannot save anyone from Life and we cannot save anyone from their lessons. People attract what they need in order to learn the lessons of living. Allow the Life process to work for others just as it is working for you.

Give YourSelf A Path Of Accomplishments

I'm not against the impossible dream, but you need realistic levels of accomplishment along the way. Rather than looking at the big dream, set up a series of small achievements. These achievements lead to the big dream and let you know if progress is being made. It's all more manageable and prevents the dream from becoming a source of frustration and failure.

In practical terms this means making a list of specific accomplishments for this month, next month and so on. These accomplishments must be clearly "do-able" and lead to the more abstract ideal. If you only focus on the end result you'll feel frustration, failure and a feeling of "why can't I make this happen?"

It is important that these goals be realistic, you must be able to accomplish the goal. Setting these realistic goals teaches you to recognize true potentials and abilities.

Break Away

A work break is intended to be an emotional, mental and physical breather. It is supposed to give you a little psychological distance from the activity you've been working at. It needs to be a change, different from work. The pattern of burnouts is to continue to work through the break, to vary the work and call it a break or to discuss work on the break. If you're doing this you misuse breaks and aggravate burnout.

Whatever gains are made from using a break to get a little extra work done are outweighed by the loss of energy and patience and by the increase in errors or poor judgements at the end of the day. We're far better off relaxing, listening to a meditation tape, going outside for a walk, or doing some light exercises. Get away from the pressures of work, lighten the load, shake off whatever heavy energy you've gathered and you'll be better able to cope, coming back to the work with perspective, poise and judgement. It's like having a second opinion that comes from Self.

Overtime Is Overdoing

Burnouts are famous for business lunches, scheduling evening appointments, attending meetings at lunch and taking work home to "catch up" in the evening. The result is imbalance, emotional exhaustion and growing hostility toward work, people and Self.

Try taking real breaks and turning work off when you're not at work. Just try it and see if you aren't better and more productive. Work smart, not hard without guilt because you're enjoying Life a little more. Helpers often feel guilty for being happy. Our society teaches us to feel guilty if we're having "too much fun" whatever that is. We're taught that if we're having a lot of fun we're not being mature, responsible adults. Fun is not just for kids! Fun is a birthright, without it we burn out.

Learning Ignites Passion

We learned to walk by stumbling and falling. We fell again and again and picked ourselves up, tried to walk and fell again. That is how you learned to walk. It's also the way we learned to talk. We worked to form the words and make our mouth work. We often said things imperfectly and didn't care, we were totally involved in learning.

Kids are great at Life, but as we grow older we learn embarrassment and humiliation. These are tragic lessons because they prevent us from learning. When we are afraid to fall we sometimes stop walking. We cling to the things we know, stay inside our comfort zone and slowly wither away.

We learn by trying something new, by doing it less than perfectly. We all learn the same way, that is the Life process. So allow yourSelf to stumble and even fall from time to time. Get your - I always want to be in control - ego out of your own way. Living is learning and that means risking a fall.

When we stop stretching ourselves we stop growing and we lose that child within. When was the last time you learned a new skill like roller skating or painting or water skiing? Remember the excitement, risk and adventure of learning? Do you remember the excitement of that child within?

We are students of school house Earth. I'm convinced we've come here to learn Life.

Accentuate The Positive

Helping relationships tend to have a negative bias. The problems and pain take precedence so much that you can only focus on what is wrong and ignore what is right. One way of dealing with this is to make a list of what is positive, good, pleasant and satisfying about contact with people. Remembering the good makes the bad less overwhelming.

Try making a list of positive achievements of the day, if there aren't any you aren't alive in your work. Smile at someone, share a happy moment, give someone a compliment. As Leo Buscaglia says "It costs nothing to be nice". If you want to feel happiness and Love then share it.

It is good to keep thank you letters and rewards where you can see them - the minor accolades as well as the major.

All human sharing can be replenishing. Someone venting anger is generating a positive and necessary exchange as long as you don't absorb their problem.

Seeing things as half full rather than half empty is just a thought away.

Bathing In Inspiration

The reality of the work world means that encouragement, praise and emotional support doesn't come from above. This isn't the way it needs to be, but unfortunately it's usually the way it is.

During some chapter of your Life you've encountered a motivator, a person who brings out the best in other people. This person has learned to look for strengths and potentials rather than flaws and weakness. I learned this from a friend who said "Peter everybody has an ass hole, you just have to decide whether to look at it."

Everybody has strengths and potentials and you can be a people motivator by seeing abilities and potentials in others. The rewards of helping people to discover the best parts of themselves are great.

Generating Good Feedback

You can make good feedback happen. In the professional dynamic appreciation is usually absent because you're being paid to do this, it hasn't occurred to the client that you need feedback. So ask for it! "If this helps let me know?"; "Let me know if this works out"; "I can do a better job if I know what you like about my work (as well as what you dislike)". Once people are aware it is as appropriate to compliment as to criticize they allow positive thoughts and feelings to flow through them, and they end up feeling better too.

Listen To Your Self

Tune in to inner feelings. Be sensitive to your personal reactions and reflect on the reasons for them. This ability to introspect - to stay in touch with Self, the needs of the child within you - is critical to countering burnout. You are the best instrument for gauging your wellness. If you ignore early warning signs the symptoms will grow into debilitating problems.

You can tap into your inner feelings easily. Take a couple of pieces of paper. At the top of the first page write *I am _____ because.*

Fill in the blank with what you're feeling, is it anger, fear, confusion? Depression is always repressed anger. Then relax and let your hand finish the sentence. Something like this:

I am angry because... *I am better than this*

I deserve better

I'm worth it

Let the thoughts flow onto the page. Nobody else needs to see it, so let it all go.

I do this whenever I'm emotionally upset and am always surprised at how much flows out. Then I look at the sources of anger and decide what to do about them. Often I'll come up with an action to resolve the situation and I feel instantly better. I'll also see that most things I'm carrying anger about aren't important any more so I release them.

Self communication also happens with a diary, talking into a tape recorder or talking it out with a supportive colleague or friend. What you're doing is giving form to the emotion, understanding what it is about rather than letting it fester inside.

The Trouble Log

If you have a persistent symptom, like headaches, lower back pain or insomnia you can use the trouble log to monitor your emotional stress.

Trouble Log

stress signs	time	where, doing what with whom	thoughts or feelings	response to stress
1.				
2.				
3.				
4.				

Try the Trouble Log for two weeks and look for patterns, possible causes, your reactions and coping mechanisms.

Coffee is not a good coping mechanism, it is not good fuel. It is a drug. Coffee is like doubling the voltage in a child's toy. For a while it runs really fast but it doesn't take long before it overheats and the wiring and motor burn out.

The trouble log will help you understand the whys of burnout and find appropriate actions. Knowing that certain times of the day are problematic you can schedule low stress activities for those times, or schedule a break like taking a walk instead of staying at your desk or going for coffee. Continued health, wealth and well being can only be based on an informed understanding of Self.

Be Constructive, Not Destructive

Self analysis is constructive not destructive. Nobody wants to know what you are against, we want to know what you are for. You don't need Self criticism, your Self is wonderful, it's your negative choices that aren't. Beating yourSelf up for your flaws is not the same as looking for ways to be better. Recognize your humanity and build on it. Remember, we always do the best with what we have to work with and you're accumulating a lot more to work with. The fact you've read this far into the book is evidence you're open and ready for growth and change.

Working Smart

When we're in water over our head we either tense, panic and drop under the surface, or relax, make a stroke and swim.

When we're overwhelmed and drowning at work, a common response is to tense and work even harder in an attempt to catch up and maintain control. We do the same things, only more of them. That means arriving earlier and staying later, seeing more people with problems, doing more paperwork, laying more pressure on and pressing your nose even more tightly against that old grindstone.

The messages from Self can increase, imbalance tips the scales, stress levels rise, emotional exhaustion begins, the personal Life suffers, cynicism taints awareness and before you know it, some coping mechanism like caffeine, drugs or alcohol creeps in.

To get ahead you've lost your head, lost your values and fallen behind.

Working harder is generally not the best way - but working smarter is. That means making changes in the way you handle the job, looking for tasks other people can do, so that you do what you're most passionate about. This means that when you assume a new responsibility you release an old one.

Working smarter means doing things to streamline the work, finding ways to get things done as easily as possible.

When you are driving your car and approach a steep hill, it's better to shift down to a lower gear than to just give it more gas at a high gear.

Get Over YourSelf

We're programmed to see the flaws in things. The education system teaches us to compare ourselves, to rate ourselves on a multitude of scales and to constantly appraise and measure and compete. How do I look, how does she look. Am I good enough, smart enough, rich enough?

Ugh!

We vividly remember the humiliations and embarrassments of our lives, the perceived failures and weaknesses that the self-sabotaging tyrant throws back into our mind every time we need confidence. I have a tape program that deals with the tyrant part of you.

Am I enough? Are you enough? ... We're enough! We're great, and the architect that created us doesn't make any junk. This society creates junk, A LOTTA JUNK! But you and I are not man made. Some far wiser architect created you and you aren't junk.

You only feel like trash when you're trashing.

Get Ego Out Of Your Way

The happiest and most loving people I know are without ego. They are open, aware, loving and alive. They accept themSelf as a human being with human foibles, needs and expectations. They forgive themselves for being human, realizing that's all they're ever going to be and that's good enough. They are good at Life because they're not afraid to be themSelf and allow other people to be themselves. They realize that other people's choices and challenges are theirs and the only time someone else's pain becomes yours is when you're standing too close, not allowing them their Life process.

Everyone is dealing with something all the time. At this moment everyone has an issue they are either resolving or resisting. That's Life!

You can become angry with the fact you've lessons to learn or you can smile, relax and learn Life.

The Worst Possible Scenario

What can possibly go wrong? Lets think about all the terrible things that could happen today. People you love could be hurt or killed, your pet could be run over, your heart could stop, your brain could explode, you could wet your pants at any moment. It could happen, your bladder could let go, it could just give up and leave you sitting in a puddle! It could happen and if you think about it enough it will happen. Thoughts are things, what you think you manifest. So be careful what you think. Only fill your mind with positive thoughts.

When I was designing my Discovering Potentials seminar I had fifteen hours of exercises and materials to share with people. I looked at all this great information I'd gathered, then I dropped into worst possible scenario mode. What if I leave something out? What if I forget my place and don't know what to say next? How awful if I forget a whole section. What *if* I leave something out; hmmm. I guess the sun would come up tomorrow, and Life would go on and I would still be a worthwhile person even if I did leave something out. I'd be a lot more worthwhile to have shared what I did share, than to not share anything because I might leave something out. BUT WHAT IF I FORGET WHERE I AM AND I STAND THERE NOT KNOWING WHAT'S NEXT?!!

This was a scenario that required Worst Possible Scenario explosives   I said "I choose peace", relaxed and imagined myself teaching the seminar to all of the people who were signed up to come. I imagined myself losing my place, lost in space, then I watched what happened.

In my visualization I looked at the people and said "So, what do you want me to talk about now?" The people chuckled recognizing what they'd all experienced before. Someone prompted me and I had the next topic of discussion. It didn't seem so bad, not bad at all.

Before the first seminar I filled my mind with thoughts that were positive and the seminar went without a hitch. In fact it was very, very successful. The second seminar went very well but toward the end of the last full day my train of thought derailed. I had been in the middle of something but what was it?

Eighty eyes were looking at me waiting for the rest, but the rest of what? "What was I just talking about?" I said.

The roof did not cave in. Mother Earth did not open up and swallow me. Someone in the group reminded me of what I was talking about. "I just had another thought that I'll share with you in a moment, it was about the mind being like an art gallery and we hang up the pictures. And you make the galleries of your mind beautiful or ugly". I looked at the person who'd prompted me and asked her to prompt me about galleries of the mind.

I then continued with the first point and came back to the second one and learned a wonderful lesson that has liberated me from any fears or problems with speaking to any sized group. Everyone wants me to be successful. I can establish rapport with any audience by allowing them to participate so we set up a conversational atmosphere rather than a lecture. And I learned what every stand up comic has to develop, I learned to play with an audience, to be a free thinker and follow the moment and see where it takes us. And the result is always something fresh, exciting and right for the moment.

I have a friend who is a talented chiropractor and a natural teacher. He has many things to share and he'd wanted to teach seminars but the idea that he might forget something or lose his place prevented him from sharing all the wonderful things he has to share. After seeing me teach and play and have fun with people he began doing his seminars and many people have benefitted.

Worst possible scenarios can paralyze you. Play with them and you'll see that whatever can go wrong isn't all that bad if we stay human and be our Self. People who think they have to be totally professional and together in every moment are far from together because they've fragmented their professional self from their personal self. Getting it together is allowing yourSelf to flow through you all the time and realizing that Self is the best part of you.

Choose Peace

Is the challenge of the day your stumbling block or your stepping stone? Will you let it pull you down or lift you up?

You decide, you always have.

It can feel like a war going on inside. Thoughts and feelings are doing battle, your mind doesn't slow down and it's more crazy inside you than it is outside you.

Nothing needs to take you down if you choose peace. It may sound too simple to be real, but returning to a state of peace is not complicated, it doesn't require external devices, it simply requires a moment of releasing the forms around you and choosing peace within.

The next time you're mentally, emotionally or physically strung out, let that child within you take you to a quiet, nurturing place. It may be a park an art gallery, a roof top.

Wander to a nurturing place. Sit down take a few long, deep breaths and say the words, *I choose peace*. Feel the words. *I choose peace. I choose peace.*

If you feel a loving wash of energy that bathes you in a feeling of lightness you're with thousands of other people who choose peace and get it.

Your subconscious, your spirit/Self, is always listening and reacting to what you are choosing to do with your thoughts. Be careful what you ask for from yourSelf, because you'll get it.

Choose peace on a regular basis and enjoy feeling your inner wisdom, your sense of better judgement and your spiritual connections. Thoughts, decisions and responses come from within. Know this and work *with* the process. The ultimate answers of your Life are not outside you, only the clues are.

Take Things Less Personally

Eighty percent of the time when someone is venting anger at you, you are absolutely not responsible for their anger. People who deal with people are open to receiving anger, fear, pain or guilt. Negative thoughts and emotions are real things they have real characteristics, vibrations and tendencies. Being in a uniform, in a helping profession, behind a counter or just being in the line of fire makes you a mark. We've all had it happen, we're feeling just fine and someone comes along, vents their anger and we carry it for them the rest of the day.

Now that you're aware emotions are real things that can be spread around to other people, you're better equipped to see it coming. You know the signs, the tight red face, tense muscles, back a bit arched, hands clenched in fists and lots of loud talking or yelling.

It isn't about you, it is about yesterday, this morning or their responses to Life in general. Don't absorb other people's garbage.

How To Stay Clear

Her are five great techniques for not carrying other people's baggage.

1. **Protect YourSelf** with your own aura. As soon as someone approaches you with anger, think the words *I choose peace...I block their energy*. Imagine yourself setting up an impenetrable light shield and concentrate on maintaining this shield until the negativity stops flying. Once the person has vented, they'll calm down.

Our first response to anger is usually to become weak or vulnerable because this is what we did when we were scolded by parents. Like a scolded puppy that rolls over on its back, we open and let it all in. Or we mirror the anger and use the opportunity to vent anger right back at the person. Anger doesn't work.

The anger you get from other people is almost always a response to what happened to them earlier that day, last night or yesterday. It's most likely about something that has nothing to do with you. It is almost never your fault, so don't let their crap inside you.

Stay centered and affirm what you want from the situation.

Many people carry a parent's emotional baggage their entire life. Don't do it!

2. **Things Are Looking Up**. It is impossible to stay angry when you are looking up. A wonderful architect has designed us and this is one of the hidden options. We can't stay angry when we're looking up.

As you set up your protective shield look up and say I choose peace. This protects you and the other person will start to wonder what the heck you're looking at. They start to look up too. And on a base level they'll realize you aren't a porter of pain, you don't carry other people's emotional baggage. They'll calm down.

3. **The Pattern Break** is a great technique. When someone is in a rage the anger is flowing out of them, they're releasing and purging and the release is probably very necessary so let them release, but wait for your opportunity to interject with the pattern break- a stunning comment very different from the person's rage energy. Keep in mind you've got your protective shield up and you're checking out the ceiling. Then, when they're pausing to catch a breath say "How is this behavior working for you?" Then make eye contact, letting them know you're ready to listen.

I've also been know to say "That color looks great on you." They're stunned, they think I'm nuts. They just tried to dump pain into me and I'm looking at the ceiling smiling and THEN I tell them I like their outfit!

I don't carry other people's excess baggage. They've got to learn to choose peace, to choose Love rather than anger or fear. Anger never gives us what we want, which is to be loved and accepted.

4. **Blow It Off**. If you do happen to absorb someone else's pain, or if they stir up a little pain you've been carrying around, get rid of it. Relax and imagine yourself with a balloon. Think of yourself blowing up this imaginary balloon with all the anger, all the bad feelings. Fill up that balloon, fill it up with everything you do not like. Stretch that balloon to the limit, then tie it off. Then toss this balloon up and up and send it into the light so the bad feelings will never return to you.

5. **Crying On Your Mother's Breast**. Here is another technique one of my seminar coordinators was taught by a shaman.

Relax yourself and imagine you are in a forest. Dig a hole to put all your anger into. Then put your face over the hole and shout all your feelings, all the thoughts and hurts and anger into that hole. It's O.K. Mother Earth is big enough to take it. Shout and cry and send those feelings down into the soil.

Then, when the feelings have been vented, take a seed from a nearby tree and plant it into the hole. Cover the seed, thank your mother Earth for offering you her flesh for your hurt and walk away knowing that something beautiful always grows from pain.

If you aren't good at imagining, go outside somewhere, dig the hole and do it. Better you let mother Earth take it than the parent of your child or your child.

Dealing With The Dysfunctional

Being a caregiver can sometimes feel like staying too long at a smorgasbord. We've got to pay attention to when we've had enough.

We all encounter people who are lazy, irresponsible, rude, belligerent and even threatening. You may be encountering people who aren't ready to change, the pain hasn't gotten bad enough for them to change, yet the social system is shoving them at you for fixing.

People will not change until they are ready. They can be banging their head against that wall, you can show them the door, but until they decide the door is better they won't use it. You could push them through the door but when people are pushed they usually lose their way. We're all finding our own way through the mazes of Life. Would you want to be pushed?

Encouragement and instilling Self confidence are positive, loving things to do, but pushing doesn't work.

Allow people their pain, allow people their process and you spare yourself a lot of pain.

If you see people as the amazing and wonderful reactions to Life that they are, you can forgive people for who they are. I absolutely know that we all do the best with what we have to work with.

Pain Is A Path

We need to hurt, we need pain. Pain is Life's great teacher. If you try to spare someone else their pain you are not helping them. They need the pain in order to change and learn to be better at Life.   They need the pain to become so unbearable that they will change.

You can absorb other people's pain. You can take it and carry it around for them but you are not helping them or yourSelf. Be a loving and caring teacher, recognize their situation but don't attempt to absorb their pain or carry it away. If you do you deny them their lesson and prolong their pain. The pain has to get bad enough before they'll change and make it better.

Life is a very interesting school. We're all learning something. I am, you are, everyone is. True, you may see someone struggling with the most elementary lesson that you learned decades ago. You can share your story with them, you can show them the door that led out of pain for you, but they must choose to use the door and your door may not be their door.

We're all on a Life journey during which there are peaks and valleys. Very little grows on the peaks but lots of things grow in the valleys.

Don't deny anyone their Life lessons. Take a look at yourSelf and see what lessons you have before you. Many caregivers are frantically healing others in order to avoid healing themSelves.

Moving From Believing To Knowing

Another technique I've taught to the hundreds of people who've taken my seminar is to ask your Self "What do I want"? Listen for your answer. Then ask again, "What do I want?" Listen, and ask one more time. By doing this you're making decisions internally. It is a major step toward beating burnout.

But the step goes one further. After asking what you want three times and listening for the answer you might also ask "What is of the highest good", and listen for the answer. The highest good takes other people and the whole Universe into account.

What you're doing here is learning your true wants, so you're communicating with yourSelf now and living for yourSelf and your wants and needs. You're also looking at the whole situation and asking what is of the highest good for all. This takes people, money and organization into account. This is a powerful way of making decisions. Inner conflicts are eliminated and you are in line with your true wants and the highest good. Burnout is avoided again.

The Power Of Love

There is one thing every living thing responds to, the one thing we want above all, Love. If you allow yourself to Love the people you encounter, to give them Loving and caring thoughts and actions, they will respond. It may take time for them to "get it" but they will.

We all want the same things, to be Loved and accepted. Unconditional Love has no strings attached. It is given with no expectations of return and the giver seeks ways to give again. This is unconditional Love.

Loving someone means allowing them to be who they are. If they are harming other people they need to be restricted until they learn their behavior doesn't work. But for the most part people, like lovers, need to be given Loving thoughts and the best information we can share, then they need to be set free. When they are ready they'll get IT.

Life is IT, and you and I are on our path of learning getting IT too.

Relaxation

Tense muscles, high blood pressure an upset stomach are some ways the body tells us we're not getting Life right. Not only are the symptoms unpleasant but they lead to serious health problems. Reduction of these health problems can be achieved by learning how to relax physically and mentally.

Relaxation techniques come in various forms and a multitude of labels. Meditation, biofeedback, transcendental meditation, yoga, Silva Method, self-hypnosis - these labels all apply to the same physical state. When we give ourSelf instructions to relax we do. It is as simple as that. You can use deep breathing, visualizations or any number of techniques which will change your brain wave pattern from Beta to the relaxed state of Alpha. Your body easily follows your mind into the relaxed state. Closing your eyes and visualizing yourSelf in a relaxed environment, walking on a beach, fishing, sitting by a stream, your most relaxing thoughts, will also relax you.

These relaxation techniques can be easily used at your desk, during breaks, and before a potentially stressful event.

My Beating burnout audio cassettes will teach you relaxation techniques to release heavy emotions, lose anxiety, forgive and heal.

A Word of Warning About Relaxation

Stress symptoms are an indication of an overloaded system. Relaxation techniques can remove the symptoms but if the source is not dealt with you will burn out. Treating the symptom is not treating the cause, so treat the cause and the symptom at the same time.

In case studies with nurses the relaxation techniques resolved the symptoms well. But a follow-up found that nurses using the relaxation techniques were having the most problems. They'd learned to relax, interpreted the lack of stress as an indication of strength and were taking on more responsibilities and working harder. Instead of alleviating stress the relaxation response exacerbated it.

Listen to your body, allow yourself to change and eliminate sources of burnout while learning to relax.

Decompress After Work

Bringing home the burnout burns out your home. You need to think of work and home as two very different environments. A transition is needed to get from one to the other and the double martini is not the best transitional tool.

When I was certified as a SCUBA diver I learned about decompression. Below thirty feet the diver experiences high atmospheric pressure. If the diver returns too quickly to the surface's normal atmospheric pressure, nitrogen bubbles can be released into the bloodstream causing a painful and possibly paralyzing condition called the "bends".

To avoid this the diver must make a gradual transition from the depths to allow the body to decompress. In a similar way you need to decompress from the high pressure work environment into the "normal pressure" of private Life.

My Decompression tape takes you through a relaxation process after work and puts you in a "weekend" state of mind. The situations and pressures of the day are gone. Any problems are given to your subconscious to process and resolve so you can enjoy your time.

The most insidious way to let your work overrun your Life is to bring home the emotional turmoil of the day. This tape stops recurring thoughts and unresolved feelings by handing them over to your very wise subconscious. You come up from the tape feeling relaxed and without a need to burden anyone you Love.

Information on ordering Decompression and Forgiveness tapes is at the back of the book.

You can develop your own decompression techniques. I personally use my meditation tapes and working out at the gym. Keeping myself in a fit body has a multitude of benefits, some people jog, other people spend an hour reading a good, non-work related book. The best decompression activities remove you from people, giving you personal privacy and Self-indulgence. When I travel to large cities I often see commuters reading the newspaper or listening to tapes. Their commuting time in a crowded train is spent decompressing.

Here are some decompression ideas: write letters to friends, enjoy a creative hobby, take a long walk or jog, sit and daydream, lie down and meditate, soak in a hot tub, listen to relaxing 'new age' or classical music, learn a language with instructional tapes, take up a non- competitive sport. (If you choose a competitive sport like tennis, don't compete, play.)

For my money, the best place to decompress is Nature. This is where we can ground ourselves, stay close to the Earth and Be. I live in places with tall beautiful trees and water nearby. I need these elements in my Life. A walk by the river and a sit at the base of a tree is one of the best ways I know to decompress.

Change The World Or Change Your Self

Since burnout sets in when effort spent is in inverse proportion to the reward received, it is imperative to balance the equation.

This book is about helping yourSelf. Once you are on firm ground with Self you are in a power position to change "the system". That can mean changing an organization, making it a better place to be, a more human and nurturing experience, and it always begins by changing your reaction to the situation and realizing that each individual is responsible for their Life. When a teacher accepts there will always be quick students, slow students, easy students and angry students in every class, that person becomes a forgiving teacher and a loving student. Whenever we work with people, forgiveness and Love are the only things that will sustain us. People are the challenge and the reward.

You have tremendous, infinite power over all Life because your total awareness of Life is a perception within you. If you want to change the world, change yourSelf.

Once you feel good about you, then you can change things outside you.

By using the solutions offered in this book, you are moving toward empowering yourSelf.

You do have power over every situation but the true power is in your response. Respond with anger and you are weak, respond with Love and you get positive results. For instance if you see your boss as a nasty, ineffective, miserable power monger you are not in a position of influence.

If you look for the child within that boss, remembering everyone wants to be loved and accepted, understanding replaces anger and fear, positions and status are negated and you recognize your boss as a person who is angry and afraid and also has lessons to learn.

By changing your perception you see things clearly, and you are in a position of positive influence. Simply stated you are coming from Love rather than anger or fear.

Suddenly you realize that your supervisor's problems aren't yours or your fault. You no longer need to absorb his or her emotional garbage and your responses will naturally change.

When you are weak, angry or burnt out you won't be listened to. When you're aware, strong and passionate again, you'll be in a position of power... real power because you'll understand positive change.

Quitting Your Job

If, in spite of following many of my recommendations, the job situation has not improved, it may be time for you to make a move. You may be working for a burnout manager or a burnout business in which there is never enough, in which you can't win.

Quitting a job is high stress, it has psychological and financial impact. Before giving up your job, examine the underlying reasons and the available alternatives.

If you are thinking of quitting, make a list of the reasons this job is draining you. Make this list now.

☆

Now take a look at the list and see if it is the job or your handling of the situation that is causing burnout. Is it them or is it you?

In the new job there will always be Them and there will always be You. Even if you're going to be self employed, you're still counting on customers and clients.

Change does not automatically guarantee success. So look at where you've been and where you want to go and plan this change well. You can make this a positive step. It can be much better, but make your expectations realistic and anticipate complications and challenges.

If you've had another offer get it in writing, and get the things you need guaranteed in writing. This way you know where you're going and the stress of this change is lessened.

Going into the same job situation and handling it the same way as before does not represent progress. Many burnouts close their eyes, say I want outta here and go into another situation with their eyes and mind still closed.

A well planned change is great! But planning involves taking honest stock of the situation and yourSelf in order to take better care of yourSelf. Know what you need and make the changes.

Power Verses Powerlessness

Burnout is a greater risk when people feel weak or unassertive, trapped by other people's demands, feeling , held down and boxed in by institutional regulations and the endless demands of the people they serve. Feeling at the mercy of the situation, having to surrender yourSelf to the job every day is a state in which passion can't survive.

Many of the techniques for beating burnout are strategies for personal power, awareness of Truth and the spiritual side of Life. We need an awareness that the society that we live in conspires against the individual.

Getting from one end of a career to the other can be like walking a path dotted with land mines. If you Love and nurture yourSelf, your instincts and Self preservation tools are activated and you can much better avoid the land mines.

If you over commit yourself to being Normal, to the organization and the job role, rules and regulations, you're committing yourself to such an unreliable fickle force that you're almost bound to burn out. A sense of humor and awareness of the absurd are common senses uncommonly used. Don't lose your sense of humor.

Since burnout sets in when effort spent is in inverse proportion to the reward received, it is imperative to balance the equation.

This book is about helping yourself. That can mean changing your organization, making it a better place to be, a more human and nurturing experience, but a great deal of it means changing you. As the solutions in this book suggest.

Once you are on firm ground with yourSelf you are in a power position to change "the system".

You have tremendous... infinite power over your Life. You are a powerful being in a sea of energy. You determine how you row your boat on the stream. Try living gently, merrily and see if things aren't better.

By using these solutions you are empowering yourSelf. You're reviewing your Life and finding out what you want to change about you. Once this is done successfully you are in a position to effect change in the situation around you. You do have power over every situation but you need to be in a position of knowing, of personal strength to effect positive change in your work environment. When you are weak you won't be listened to. When you're strong and passionate again, you'll be in a position of power, real power because you'll understand change.

Organizations must realize the importance of a person's sense of identity and Self-worth. Organizations must humanize and manage people. Again; the essence of managing is to give employees what they need to be excellent at what they do. That means the tools, the education, the motivation, the praise and the freedom to find better ways of doing it.

When a person doesn't feel he or she has an impact on the process, the flames of passion are seriously dampened.

Life is a solitary experience in a group setting. The individual is ultimately responsible for the Self. Beating burnout begins and ends with nurturing the Self and making wise choices for the highest good. In this increasingly unhuman society each person must focus their awareness upon humanity.

The directors of institutions must turn their energies toward people and enhance each workers sense of personal accomplishment, passion and desire to do the job.

I think we will enter the 21st Century regarding time more as a gift to be appreciated and less as an opportunity to be exploited. But in the 90s, the burnout decade, things will get worse before we'll get better.

Institutions are dead things, they do not breathe, they are dinosaurs. But the directors of institutions are people, the employees are people and the products are for people.

We must humanize our lives. We must humanize our society.

♡

Bibliography

Dyer, Dr. Wayne, "You'll See It When You Believe It", New York: William Morrow & Company Inc. 1989.

Hanson, Dr. Peter, "The Joy Of Stress", Toronto: Hanson Stress Management Organization, 1985.

Hanson, Dr. Peter, "Stress For Success", Toronto: Collins Publishers, 1989.

Hay, Dr. Louise L., "You Can Heal Your Life", Santa Monica: Hay House, Inc. 1984.

McGugan, Peter, "A Journey To The Soul" Video, London Canada: Journey Productionns & Potentials Press, 1989.

Moody, Dr. Raymond A. , "Life After Life" , New York: Bantam Books, 1976.

Padus, Emrika, "The Complete Guide To Your Emotions And Your Health", Emmaus Pennsylvania: Rodale Press, 1986.

Pines, Ayala & Aronson A., "Career Burnout Causes & Cures", New York: Macmillin Inc. , 1988.

Pines, Ayala & Aronson A., "Burnout, From Tedium to Personal Growth", New York: Macmillin Inc. , 1980.

Welch, David & Medeiros, Donald & Tate, George, "Beyond Burnout", Englewood Cliffs New Jersey: Prentice-Hall, Inc. 1982.

Index

The most complete program of its kind.
8 audio cassette programs for losing anxiety, reducing pain,
enhanced healing, wellness through the mind, releasing
negativity & forgiveness

'I wrote and created the wellness tapes to help people use their
inner abilities for healing. They've been particularly successful
for people challenged by cancer and AIDS.'

Peter McGugan

Canada / P.O. 24042, London, Ontario N6H 5C4
U.S./ P.O. 635, Lake Orion Michigan 48305

Enclose a cheque or money order for $39.95

About the Author

Peter McGugan B.A., H.B.J., Ct. H.

LECTURER, HUMORIST, AUTHOR, BROADCASTER,
HYPNOTHERAPIST, PSYCHOLOGIST

Peter McGugan has had a hectic and varied career as a network television reporter, a producer, an author and therapist.

After burning out twice he was told, due to a progressive case of osteo-arthritis, he would probably live out his life in a wheelchair.

This revelation prompted his return to the study of psychology. After realizing there wasn't a good system to help people diagnose themselves and beat burnout, Peter decided to create one. The result is this book, audio tapes, a feature length video and an extremely successful series of speeches and seminars.

Peter McGugan continues to enthrall audiences with his humorous, sensitive and touching appreciation of the human condition in the 90s.

From a victorian cottage in picturesque London, Ontario he oversees his private clinic, supervises the production and distribution of his books and tapes, travels to do speeches and seminars and fully enjoys what he calls "a fantastic Life".

Compared to when he used to burn out, his creativity and productivity have doubled. He still jogs every day and is a living testimony that Beating Burnout works.

Responses to Peter's Speeches and Seminars

"Excellent, informative, entertaining and thought provoking...positive responses from all attendees. I'm recommending you highly."
Peter McGillivary V.P. RE/MAX Canada

"Simply the best, most entertaining speaker of the year."
Dave Pollick, London Ad & Sales Club

"Thank you, you helped make our conference a huge success, everyone loved your presentation."
Dr. Anne Spencer,
Intl. Medical & Dental Hypnotherapy Association

"The response to your presentation was very positive... your quality and leadership contributed greatly to our success".
Patti Etkin, OPTIMA Health Conference 1990

"I thank you for the very funny and moving presentation... right on the mark."
Joan Ball, Canadian Mental Health Association

"It is the most important seminar I've ever attended, and believe me I've been to more than I can remember."
Betty Chanyi, Teacher

"Peter does a splendid job of covering all aspects of the burnout problem."
Dr. Irene Hickman, Physician, Author

For information on speeches and seminars contact us at
P.O. Box 24042
London, Ontario Canada N6H 5C4
or call (519) 645-0884

ORDER FORM

	Price	Quantity	Total
Audio			
Forgiveness & Losing Anxiety	12.00		.
Decompression & Creativity	12.00		.
Video			
A Journey To The Soul	29.95		.
Books			
Beating Burnout: the survival guide for the 90s	12.00		.
		Order Total	.

Canada/ P.O. 24042, London, Ontario   N6H 5C4

U.S. /   P.O. 635, Lake Orion, Michigan   48361

Enclose a cheque or money order.

Please Print

NAME _____

ADDRESS _____   CITY _____   ZIP _____   U.S.A.____ CANADA____

Tapes, Books & Seminars

Audio Cassettes
Forgiveness & Losing Anxiety: This very popular tape teaches you to deeply relax and takes you through an easy forgiveness process. The losing anxiety side allows you to release tensions and tightness to program yourself for what you desire and either drift into sleep or come up feeling refreshed and invigorated.

Decompression & Creativity: The decompression program teaches you to deeply relax and release tensions and stress after working. The issues of the day are turned over to your subconscious and you either drift into sleep or come up feeling refreshed and invigorated.

Video -VHS
'A Journey To The Soul': Peter McGugan's visually stunning feature film is a video seminar. It is a great tool for beating burnout. Learn more about balancing your Life • The importance of thoughts and feelings • Fourteen normal Life experiences that may be alienating you from fulfillment and happiness • Why we may feel Love/hate toward our parents •

Books
To order more copies of "Beating Burnout: the survival guide for the 90s", use the order form on the following page. Bookseller and volume costs are available.

Seminars
If you would like information on speaking engagements and Beating Burnout seminars please request information from the shipping departments.

ORDER FORM

Audio	Price	Quantity	Total
Forgiveness & Losing Anxiety	12.00		.
Decompression & Creativity	12.00		.
Video			
A Journey To The Soul	29.95		.
Books			
Beating Burnout: the survival guide for the 90s	12.00		.
		Order Total	.

Canada/ P.O. 24042, London, Ontario   N6H 5C4

U.S./ P.O. 635, Lake Orion, Michigan   48361

Enclose a cheque or money order.

Please Print

NAME _____

ADDRESS _____ CITY _____ ZIP _____ U.S.A. _____ CANADA _____